COLLECTOR'S GUIDE TO
ART DECO

MARY FRANK GASTON

COLLECTOR BOOKS
P.O. Box 3009
Paducah, KY 42002-3009

The current values in this book should be used only as a guide. They are not intended to set prices, which vary from one section of the country to another. Auction prices as well as dealer prices vary greatly and are affected by condition as well as demand. Neither the Author nor the Publisher assumes responsibility for any losses that might be incurred as a result of consulting this guide.

To Vera
who lived the era

Other Books By Mary Frank Gaston

The Collector's Encyclopedia of Limoges Porcelain $19.95

The Collector's Encylcopedia of R.S. Prussia, First Series $24.95

The Collector's Encyclopedia of R.S. Prussia, Second Series $24.95

Blue Willow, An Illustrated Value Guide . . . . $ 9.95

The Collector's Encyclopedia of Flow Blue China $19.95

Haviland Collectables and Objects of Art $19.95

American Belleek $19.95

Antique Brass . . . . $ 9.95

Antique Copper . . . . $ 9.95

The titles may be ordered from the author or the publisher. Include $1.00 each for postage and handling.

Mary Frank Gaston
P.O. Box 342
Bryan, TX 77806

Collector Books
P.O. Box 3009
Paducah, KY 42001

Acknowledgments

Several individuals and businesses assisted with this project. With few exceptions, photographs were taken at antique shops or shows where it was not always convenient to work. Dealers were very cooperative, however, whether it was necessary to rearrange displays or take items out of booths to another location where there was more room or better light for taking photographs. They graciously helped in any way, sharing their knowledge and expertise. Their enthusiasm and enjoyment in dealing with Art Deco was obvious, making this particular task a delightful experience. I offer my most sincere appreciation to the following:

Barbara and Pete Nicholson, Joaquin, Texas (formerly Art Deco Adventure, Austin, Texas)

Jake Iseman and Dane Hawkins, Justaposition, Houston, Texas

The Thomas M. Crocker Collection

Dee's Uniques, Etc., Jefferson, Texas

Bobby G. Green, The Past Revisited, Abilene, Texas

I would also like to thank The Antique Center, San Antonio, Texas; The Antique Connection, San Antonio, Texas; Dorothy Ball, El Paso, Texas; C & M Enterprises, Houston, Texas; The Depot, New Braunfels, Texas; The Doubletree, Wimberly, Texas; George H. Dreyfus, L'Opera Antiques, Austin and Beauvais, France; David Harris, Big D Bazaar, Dallas, Texas; Dianne Heath, Salmagundi, Amarillo, Texas; David F. Ledbetter, Yesterdaze Mall, Abilene, Texas; House of Lowell, Houston, Texas; B. Lightsey, San Antonio, Texas; Mrs. J.C. McElvain, Dallas, Texas; The Main Place, San Antonio, Texas; Rosie O'Reilly, Austin, Texas; Fay Schoenfeld, San Antonio, Texas; The Uncommon Market, Dallas, Texas; and The Victory Antiques, Dallas, Texas.

Finally, I thank three people who have always been instrumental in the books I have written. My husband, Jerry, also a Deco fan, photographed all of the pieces illustrated and always assists me in ways too numerous to mention. My editor, Steve Quertermous, is constantly behind the scenes ensuring a smooth transition from typed pages and bundles of pictures to a completed book. My publisher, Bill Schroeder, Collector Books, by publishing this survey and giving me another opportunity to work on a most interesting subject.

Preface

As a child of the 1940's, I grew up during the waning years of what is now called the Art Deco period. Various and sundry remnants from that past which happened to linger on the scene in the way of household objects, clothing and jewelry evidently made a lasting impression on me. I always seem to have had a nostalgic interest in them. Although perhaps I was aware of "Deco" before "collecting Deco was cool," unfortunately I did not get in on the ground floor, so to speak, and capture prime examples by famous artists and designers of the era. This was because I lacked both the knowledge and the resources!

In fact, once Art Deco hit the collectibles scene during the late 1960's and early 1970's, it became rather abruptly apparent that my Deco, according to some, was not considered real Deco. My "rhythm" dancing girl pot metal lamp, red cocktail glasses with chrome stems, and especially my black glass nude ashtray would fall under the heading of "kitsch," according to some writers on the subject.

Nonetheless my interest in such items did not diminish. Over the last several years, as I have traveled around the country gathering information for other books on other topics, I have seen a dramatic increase in similar types of articles appearing on the market. This "secondary" level of Art Deco can be found at antique shops, malls and shows. By and large, examples from this market are part of the large supply of mass produced and mass marketed items made during the 1920's and 1930's. Such pieces imitated or resembled "modern" looks set forth in Europe during the second quarter of the twentieth century. Many were made in the United States by various china, glass and metal companies. Deco stereotypes of angular shapes, geometric patterns, nude figures and bold colors characterize most pieces. These qualities, rather than a particular company name or manufacturer, are sought by the average collector.

An abundant supply of a large variety of articles is available. Prices have increased over the last several years as more and more collectors joins the ranks of Deco enthusiasts. Prices remain moderate, however, compared to prices obtained at the great auction houses for work by major designers and craftsmen of the period.

This book is not meant to be a literary reconstruction or detailed history of the period and its major contributors. That type of study has been very well done by others, especially Victor Arwas' *Art Deco*, Bevis Hillier's *Art Deco*, and Katherine Morrison McClinton's *Art Deco: A Guide for Collectors*. These books, as well as several other entries listed in the Bibliography, should be read by all Deco collectors.

This survey centers on the type of Deco currently found for sale at general antique and collectibles outlets. While most are representative of mass productions, some pieces by noted "names" of the period are sometimes found in such locations. I have included examples by French designers and manufacturers such as Sandoz, Daum and Sabino because they were available for sale and thus do comprise part of the average market place.

The 318 color photographs are divided into ten categories of Art Deco collectibles. Each section is prefaced with brief introductory remarks about the category itself and some of the pieces featured. A Value Guide corresponding to the numbers of the photographs is also included. The Object and Manufacturer Indexes help locate examples of a particular item or company. I hope you, too, enjoy Deco for the fun of it!

Mary Frank Gaston
P.O. Box 342
Bryan, TX 77806

For all correspondence, please include a self-addressed, stamped envelope.

Contents

Origins & Development of Art Deco

L'Exposition International des Arts Décoratifs et Industriels Modernes was held in Paris, France, from April to October in 1925. This international exhibit was arranged for the purpose of showing the work of current artists, craftsmen and designers who attempted to project a view of contemporary and future trends in artistic decoration. The event had been planned much earlier, but the onset and aftermath of World War I caused the Exposition to be postponed until 1925. As the title implied, the purpose of the Exposition was to demonstrate that elements of art and industrial techniques could be combined as applied art to make both utilitarian and attractive products. These were desirable to accommodate the changing life styles occurring because of the industrial progress of the 20th century.

Countries which participated at the Expostion set up pavilions to house the respective displays of their selected artisans. In addition to France, Austria, Belgium, Czechoslovakia, Denmark, England, Greece, Holland, Italy, Japan, Monaco, Poland, Russia, Spain, Sweden and Turkey were represented. Two major countries did not participate. Germany was not invited because of the strained relations resulting from the war. The United States did not accept the invitation because according to ''Herbert Hoover . . . there was no modern art in the United States'' (Arwas, p. 14). For a full description of the 1925 Exposition, see the book by Frank Scarlett and Marjorie Townley (*Arts Décoratifs 1925*, London: St. Martins Press, 1975).

The 1925 Exposition captured the current world of design and had a profound influence on design over the succeeding years. The styles and designs of the work shown at the Exposition were not identical. As years passed, the styles displayed in 1925 were emulated, but they were not copied slavishly or duplicated precisely. In fact, varied interpretations and other innovative designs emerged during the following years. The style highlighted in 1925 served as the basis for developing the ''modern'' look of the decorative arts over the next generation.

Because of assorted opinions about Art Deco, its history is controversial. Numerous individuals and groups, various schools of design, many social and world events, and several philosophical ideas or ''isms'' are considered instrumental in the development of Art Deco. A wealth of material has been written on these various aspects of the subject. It is not my purpose to present a detailed historical survey. Rather, readers are encouraged to consult the selected entries in the Bibliography for a thorough review of Art Deco's complex background.

Rarely does a consensus exist about the precise dates of artistic or historical periods. Prior developments are important and will inevitably lead to some point that later is identified as the beginning of the period. The literature which describes the development of the Art Deco style has several different views about when the era began and ended and about where and why it originated. There is even disagreement about what Art Deco actually is.

Art Deco is sometimes seen as a reaction against Art Nouveau, the immediately preceding period of decorative design (1890's-1914). Art Nouveau is a style based on romantic and naturalistic images, dominated by a graceful, curvilinear line. It is highly decorative, having a sensuous, dreamy, more subtle quality than the gaudy ornamentation typically associated with the Victorian period.

Art Deco, in contrast, is often considered as an interpretation of the future based on the use of straight angles and clean lines without superflous decoration. This opinion is contradicted by observers who point out that early Art Deco did not fit that description. It was neither all lines and angles nor were all examples plain and austere. These writers believe Art Deco grew out of Art Nouveau or was a refinement of that earlier style. They emphasize that early pieces often were richly executed with lavish materials and were quite luxurious.

Some authors describe Art Deco as being a ''new art'' which did not imitate previous designs. Critics of that view believe that the ''true'' Art Deco was derived from the restrained neo-classical 18th century styles. Another view is that Art Deco borrowed from cultures such as the Egyptian, African and American Indian.

In addition to the origin and characteristics of style, the original audience for Art Deco is debatable. On the one hand, it is seen as intended for the wealthy. Some experts accept only the work of the top designers and craftsmen as being representative of true Art Deco. Certain individuals who exhibited at the Paris Exposition are usually cited as the most important names associated with the style. Others insist the style was developed primarily for the middle classes. Mass produced wares which strived to imitate the ''modern'' trends of the 1920's and 1930's are scorned by some. Such examples are often lumped under the heading of ''*kitsch*,'' a German term literally defined as ''trash,'' or the debasement of original works. Today, however, many of those items have become extremely collectible and comprise the major part of many collections.

Another dispute in the literature is that Art Deco is synonymous with France. Deco items of French origin are considered superior to examples from other countries. France, in fact, is usually considered the birthplace of Art Deco, especially because of the 1925 Exposition. Yet knowledgable writers trace its development through other European centers such as Austria and Germany. Indeed, the list of countries exhibiting at the 1925 Exposition is evidence that craftsmen in many countries were designing their work simultaneously along lines which now are identified as Art Deco. Thus, it is apparent that other countries expressed their own views of modern design. And while the United States did not participate in the 1925 event, that certainly does not mean that ''modern'' design was not developing here as well.

Purists say Art Deco ended in 1925, with the peak of the style culminating in the Paris Exposition. They do not believe that the work which followed was worthy of the name. Others, less dogmatic, differentiate between ''Art Deco'' and ''Art Moderne.'' Art Deco would include design up to 1925, and Art Moderne would describe the style followed after that year and on into the 1930's. This clear division separates the components of elegant style following Art Nouveau from the purely angular and stark designs brough forth in the late 1920's.

Other critics maintain that Art Deco includes the entire period of the 1920's through the 1940's. Alternatively, Art Deco is referred to as the style popular between two World Wars—1918-1940. Other definitions of the era confine the period between the years of 1925, the date of the initial French exhibit, and 1940.

If the general consensus is that 1940 or World War II signifies the end of the main production of Art Deco, then World War I is usually considered the most important event influencing the development of the Art Deco period. Life styles certainly changed during and after the war. Servants left their positions to fight, or in the case of women, work for the war effort. The sons and daughters of the wealthy also became involved in wartime activities. After the war, many former domestics refused to return ''downstairs,'' seeking more regular jobs and their own living quarters. Because of the war, both servant class and upper class women began to become more independent. A desire to enjoy life and a relaxation of morals are also often cited as important consequences of the war. A ''middle'' class began to emerge which demanded a release from the encumbered Victorian way of life steeped in heavy traditions, pious attitudes and elaborate rituals of dressing, entertaining and running households.

Although World War I might be the focal point for recognizing a change in the world's life styles, other important factors also occurred before and after the war which helped bring about this change. The first 40 years of the 20th century witnessed unsurpassed progress in industry which led to a more convenient way of life in all areas: from horse and buggy to automobile, train and plane; from gas lighting to electricity; from outdoor to indoor plumbing; from hand delivered calling cards to telephone, telegram and radio. This period of rapid change in transportation, communication and manufacturing resulted in a smaller world, as is often quoted, by making distant people and places more accessible. But it also made the world larger for the average person by making more goods and services available and thereby allowing more individual freedom. It is not surprising that as life became more efficient, especially for the average person, all aspects of style and design were influenced.

In spite of the various views of its origin and development, Art Deco is a recognized age just as its immediate predecessors, the Victorian and Art Nouveau periods. Like those well known categories of collector interests, Art Deco, too, has become firmly established. In 1965, a revival of the 1925 Exposition, *Les Annees '25*, was held in Paris. World attention once again took a look at what had been hailed as ''modern'' in 1925. The success of this subsequent exhibit brought forth a new ''period'' for collectors. ''Art Deco,'' derived from the lengthy French title of the original Exposition, quickly caught on as an apt descriptive term not only for the style showcased in 1925, but perhaps more importantly also evolved to identify the modernistic designs which were either continued or initiated after 1925 until the 1940's.

Today, auctions specialize in sales devoted to artifacts from the period. General price guides include Art Deco as a specific entry, listing a variety of examples and current prices fetched at auctions or in the collectibles market. As collector interest in the subject grew, the definition of Art Deco has expanded to include a much broader scope than purists might prefer.

Today, Art Deco is quite loosely interpreted to include a very wide range of objects from fine art to the mundane and produced as early as the first decade of the 20th century until the beginning of the fifth decade. The style is characterized by several different elements of design which may include the following: an understated and restrained elegance; sharply angular and geometric lines, often void of any decoration; futuristic concepts; suggestions of speed and movement; both vivid and contrasting colors; Jazz age and Flapper influences; Aztec, African and Egyptian cultural symbols; and certain materials which became popular such as bakelite, celluloid, chrome and dark colored glass.

Anything which exhibits one or more of these traits is generally classified as part of the Art Deco period. It does not matter if it is an original work by a famous person or merely a mass produced dime-store novelty. Consequently, and fortunately, Art Deco can be enjoyed by collectors as diverse as its many dimensions.

Serious wealthy collectors purchase creations by top designers, artists and manufacturers identified with the early years of the era. Prices for such examples can easily mount to five figures. Many who like Deco cannot compete in that market. But as in other collecting areas, once the top of the line has been singled out and record prices paid for choice pieces, a second level of collecting surfaces which attracts a wider, though perhaps less affluent, group. Consequently, a middle ground of Deco collecting has arrived on the scene. From the offerings at shops and shows across the country, as well as a perusal of most general value surveys on the subject, interest in Art Deco with medium to moderate prices is quite strong.

While many pay thousands of dollars for Art Deco rarities and originals, perhaps seeing such purchases as investments and true works or art, there is also a growing number of enthusiasts who collect Art Deco for the fun of it! Possible future value is usually only a secondary consideration. Some might take issue with the assertion, but Art Deco is fun. Other collecting periods cannot really be characterized in that way. For instance, Victoriana is intriguing, and collectors search for the many ''necessities'' and unique items of everyday life, obsolete today, but vital at that time. Likewise, primitives are very interesting. Collectors seek the ingenuity of those individuals who had to fashion their own tools, dishes and furniture from whatever materials were at hand. Such articles may be curiosities, but they would hardly be described as ''fun.'' Most items commonly associated with Art Deco today, however, usually evoke a smile or sense of amusement because of their exaggerated lines, bold colors, ultra sophisticated or irreverent nature or cleverness of design.

The focus of this book is on a very general interpretation of Art Deco. It is intended for the collector who *enjoys* the vibrant spirit of Art Deco and who collects according to individual whimsy and moderate pocketbook, perhaps splurging at times on certain irresistible objects! Pieces illustrated include some examples by famous ''names'' with prices of over $1,000.00 but many other items are representative of the mass productions of numerous manufacturers. Those prices are certainly more now than when the articles were first produced, but they are still affordable. There are also other objects made by little known or unknown creators whose prices are quite nominal. Examples are not limited to items of French origin but include Deco from many other countries. Art Deco made in America, Czechoslovakia and Japan is especially becoming more and more popular with collectors. Concentration on Deco shapes and motifs instead of particular designers or manufacturers can often yield unexpected Art Deco treasures!

In the photographs, decorative objects for the home and personal accessories are grouped under 10 categories which comprise some of the most popular Art Deco collectibles. These categories are not meant to be comprehensive. The broad scope of the subject does not make such a survey possible. Hopefully, a sample of items in these categories will serve to suggest other Deco collecting possibilities as well as Art Deco's open ended nature. The majority of examples were available on the open market: that is, items sold at antique shops and shows rather than from private collections or museums. A price range has been established for individual items based not only on what the dealer was asking for the piece but from information gathered from numerous other sources on similar or identical pieces.

From the items featured, certain earmarks of what is currently collected as Art Deco can be seen. For instance, typical subjects of decoration are dominated by human figures either in a nude or semi-nude state, and depictions of the sun, moon and earth are prevalent. Suggestions of the future and of speed are shown either by items actually shaped in the form of an airplane, ship or rocket, or as a decorative motif.

All types of geometric shapes and lines can be found incorporated into the designs of most objects. The cube, triangle or pyramid, and stepped or zig-zagged lines are common. Crescent or half-moon shapes made into rainbows or fans, spheres representing the world, and many sundry other shapes such as a diamond, cylinder, ellipse or oval, square, hexagon and octagon stand out as well.

Repetitive, tangential, overlapping and ziggurat patterns plus juxtaposed designs appear in the design or decor of a number of pieces. Also quite noticeable are many different construction materials, ranging from ceramic, glass, ivory, marble, metals and wood to metal alloys and synthetics. From the Art Deco pictured, perhaps it will also be clear why Art Deco often is described not only by such words as chic, clever, elegant, smart, sophisticated, streamlined and tailored but also as amusing, flippant, risqué and fun!

Bar Ware

The "cocktail," derived from the French term for mixed alcoholic beverages, *coquetel,* was an integral part of the Deco era. The spirit of the fancy before-dinner mixed drink was well suited to the carefree and relaxed atmosphere of the 1920's, but its popularity endured during the troublesome years of the Depression and World War II. The custom offered escape perhaps at one point in the day from the worries at home and abroad. Today, the "cocktail hour" remains a fixed part of the social scene.

The Volstead Act (Prohibition) was passed by Americans in 1920, and the law was not repealed until 1933—13 long years. It is interesting to note that during that time, however, imbibing was anything but dormant! Home bars became a part of the modern life, from a modest card table to lavish built-in bars fitted with all the necessities for mixing and serving drinks. Of particular interest to collectors are the portable bars. These cabinets were quite compact and doubled as a piece of furniture. They were well suited to restricted living quarters. These bars were usually made of wood and designed either with open or hidden storage compartments for bottles and stemware. The portable bars usually had some space, either on top, recessed or pull out, which could be used for mixing drinks.

While the most affluent hired bartenders or butlers, the middle class host tended his own bar or allowed the guests to serve themselves. The portable bars worked well for small apartments and houses, and they are really no less useful today. French and English import houses offer a variety of styles. Prices are quite reasonable, ranging from $250 to $1,000, depending on condition and detail. Lucky is the one who finds such a bar with all of the original equipment.

A rather large variety of accessories was required to maintain a well stocked and fitted bar to accommodate ones' guests! Ice Buckets, Cocktail Shakers, Soda Dispensers, Decanters, Tumblers, Stems and Swizzle Sticks were just some of the basics. Such items also hold an interest for collectors. Because "cocktails" were actually a product of the era, the majority of bar ware items usually has some identifying characteristic associated with Deco style. In fact, to many collectors, bar ware is a particular facet of Deco.

While lending a special decor to one's entertainment center as well as a nostalgic bit of the past, bar ware accessories are often still quite usable. Many items were made either of heavy glass or chrome, both durable with non-rusting properties. Chrome was especially used for shakers, dispensers and trays. The metal with its shiny mirrored surface adapted well to the modern look. Chrome bar ware made by the Chase Company of Waterbury, Connecticut, seems to dominate the market. Examples are usually marked and prices for Chase pieces are related to the uniqueness of the object.

Wide mouthed cocktail tumblers or stems made in clear glass were fashionable during the early years, but colored glass became popular during the late 1920's and 1930's. Ruby red, cobalt blue and emerald or jade green bar glasses are eagerly sought by collectors. American Depression era glass factories contributed assorted items to this category. Colored glass combined with chrome added a smart note to bar ware items, too.

The ingenuity and creativity of bar ware manufacturers is apparent in some of the examples shown in this section. The "global" liqueur set, the "Zepplin" bar, and the "dancing nude" cocktail stem definitely define several of the preoccupations of the era—world communication, speed, relaxed morals and most of all fun! Assembling an entertaining collection of Decor bar ware can be a very enjoyable hobby.

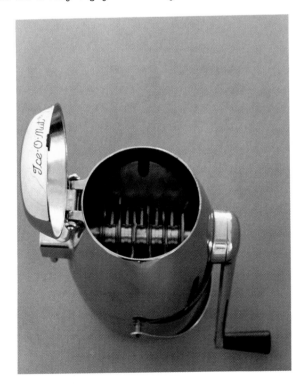

Plate 1. Ice Crusher/Bucket, 8½" h, chrome, marked "Bucketeer, Rival Mfg. Co." The "Ice-O-Mat" has a hand-turned crusher on top; the base twists off to form the bucket holder.

Plate 3. Parts of the Zepplin Bar: left to right, nested Tumblers, Cocktail Shaker, Ice Bucket; foreground, nested Stirrers and Lids for the Shaker, Ice Bucket and top cover. The container with the nested Stirrers attaches to the outer surface of the Zepplin (see preceding photograph).

Plate 2. The Zepplin Bar, chrome, 12"h, marked "Germany." The Zepplin airship was designed by the German Count, Ferdinand von Zepplin, who died in 1917. The Zepplin's futuristic shape inspired the creation of this Deco item. The following photograph shows how the Zepplin breaks down to furnish the essentials for concocting one's favorite cocktail!

Plate 4. Cocktail Set, chrome, cylinder shaped Shaker decorated with contrasting black bands at top and base; tray, 16"l; 4 wide-mouthed tumblers, 2"h, unmarked.

Plate 5. Liqueur Set, chrome, 8½"h, 14"l overall. Two spheres (globes) function as Decanters, supported on pedestal bases and fitted with spigots. The attached handle forms holder for 6 shot glasses, 4 are light blue and 2 are clear, unmarked.

Plate 7. Soda Dispenser, chrome, 9½"h, marked "Soda King, Made in USA."

Plate 6. Cocktail Shaker, chrome, 12"h, simple etched design of stylized grapes and leaves forms border on body, spout cover cork lined, unmarked.

13

Plate 8. Chrome Swan holds picks for olives and onions—basics for martinis—unmarked.

Plate 9. Cocktail Stems, ruby red glass decorated with molded geometric designs, chrome stems, 3"h, marked "Stainless Chrome," American.

Plate 10. Tumblers: left, chrome holder with cobalt blue glass insert, 2½"h; right, cobalt blue galss combined with chrome base, 3"h, unmarked.

Plate 11. Tray, 16″l, 11½″w, cobalt blue glass and chrome, attributed to American designer, Norman Bel Geddes.

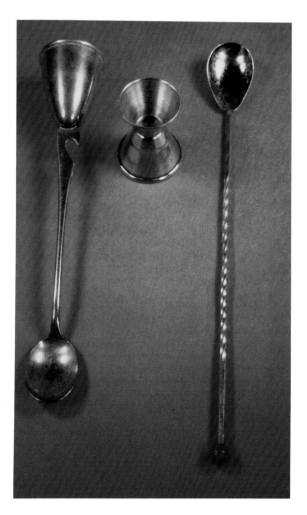

Plate 12. Assorted Bar Items: top, Stirrer, 11″l, chrome and plastic; middle, Double Jigger, 2½″h, chrome; bottom, Jigger and Stirrer combination, 9″l, silverplate.

Plate 13. Tumblers, 3″h, sterling silver, flared mouth with large round base, marked ''Cartier,'' American.

Plate 14. Cheese Board, 6½"d, wooden base, chrome cover with celluloid handle, made by Chase.

Plate 15. Cheese Dish, 14"d, chrome, made by Chase.

Plate 16. Ice Bucket, 6"h, glass, chrome handle, unmarked.

Plate 17. Ice Bucket, 11"h, chrome, unmarked; cobalt blue glass insert 8"d by Hazel Atlas, American.

Plate 18. Cocktail Stem, 5"h, dancing nude figure supports pink glass bowl, unmarked, American.

Plate 19. Cocktail Stem, 6½"h, black glass nude figure stem, clear glass bowl and base, Cambridge Glass Company, Ohio.

Plate 20. Tray and Tumblers, dark green glass, tray accented with chrome handles and holders, American.

Plate 21. Liqueur Set, amber colored glass, Decanter, 10"h, four tumblers, Czechoslovakian.

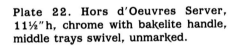

Plate 22. Hors d'Oeuvres Server, 11½"h, chrome with bakelite handle, middle trays swivel, unmarked.

Plate 23. Liqueur Set encased in replica of a bowling ball, 14"h overall, marbelized plastic, chrome dispenser, shot glasses trimmed with red, green or blue glass rings, gilded metal figure finial.

18

Clocks

Mass productions in the clock industry during the early 1800's made some type of timepiece affordable for even the most modest household. Since Victorian times, clocks have been considered a necessary as well as a decorative object. Clocks are not only useful, they also are intriguing. Their intricate works and variety of encasements have contributed to their popularity throughout the ages. Initially clocks were expensive. By the 1920's, however, the average home had more than one clock to keep everyone on time! In addition to large grandfather clocks for the hall, mantle sets and kitchen clocks, small table top varieties were made for the bedside, vanity or writing desk.

Examples in this section show how some of the prominent Deco themes were used in clock design. It is apparent that clock manufacturers were aware of the prevailing trends in home furnishings. Angular shapes, concepts of flight and motion and female or animal figures were part of the style or decoration of numerous clocks made to complement modern decor. These clocks were made from many different types of material, ranging from marble, bronze, brass and silver to wood, glass, ceramic, celluloid and plastic.

The French clocks were the most elaborate and those with figural adornments are especially sought by collectors. The figures were not always made of bronze although their finish may appear to be bronze. Metal alloys were used in the production of most available examples found today. These alloys are often referred to as pot metal, spelter or white metal. In addition to bronze colors, other color finishes were used to coat the exteriors. Such examples, however, can rarely be purchased for less than several hundred dollars. French origin and extreme or "high" Deco design account for expensive prices.

Several of the mantle sets pictured have matching side panels. These were purely decorative and served no particluar function except to flank each side of the clock. Side panels evidently have not survived all of the clocks which had them originally. While their absence does not detract from the clock itself, the panels often accentuate the overall Deco design.

Art Deco clocks can be one of the most costly categories for moderate spending collectors. Plain or less interesting specimens may still be $100 or more. Wooden shelf clocks with a simple rectangular or square shape are currently imported from abroad and may be purchased for less than $100. Beware that quite a few reproductions of Deco style clocks are also on the market. If you are interested in authentic examples from the period, check them out carefully. Most reproductions are inexpensive, have clean faces, no signs of wear on the case, and are in working condition (but many vintage ones are not!).

Plate 24. Clock, 19½"l, 16"h overall, French, marked "B. Davis, Poitiers," white onyx with grey and black marble inlaid work, decorated with bronze finished metal figures of a woman beckoning a cat. The large numbers on the face are sharply angled, and the clock's body is shaped like an Egyptian headdress.

Plate 25. Clock Set, grey and rose marble with a shape-on-shape design incorporating a diamond, circle, fan and rectangle. Clock, 13"l, 8½"h; Side Panels, 7"l, 5"h, French.

Plate 26. Clock with Side Panels, pink and white marble, semi-nude figure with stylized wings, ornamental decor made of white metal with a bronze finish, marked "Vve. Tetelin," French.

Plate 27. Clock, 15"l, 15"h, black marble and multi-colored onyx, adorned with leaping gazelles made of white metal with brown and black finish; matching Side Panels, 7"l, 6½"h, cut with steep stepped design, French.

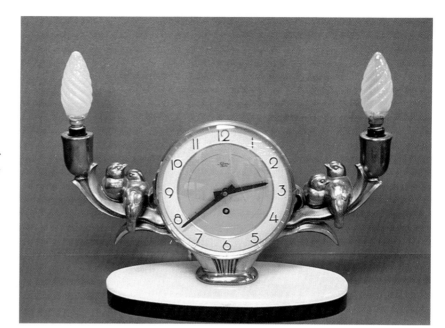

Plate 28. Electric Clock fitted with candle lights, brass, onyx, marked "Silvox, Paris," ca. 1930's.

Plate 29. Clock, 27½"l overall, reclining musician, patinated metal and composition ivory, marble base, French.

Plate 30. Digital Clock, 19"l, bronze, manufactured by Silvercrest, American, ca. mid 1930's.

Plate 31. Desk Clock, 5½"l, 4"h, bronze with black enamel trim, marked "JAZ," French, ca. 1930's.

Plate 32. Desk Clock, 8½"h, bronze case with sterling silver decorative trim, marked with Heintz Art Metal Company insignia, patent date 1912; works by Lux Clock Manufacturing, Waterbury, Connecticut.

Plate 33. Desk Clock, 4½"h, pot metal base, brass finish, triangle and stepped designs, octagonal shaped clock face, brass. The clock's base is also a bank with coin slot on reverse side.

Plate 34. Boudoir Clock, 7"h, 6"d, peach colored glass, mirrored base, American.

Plate 35. Boudoir or Vanity Clock, plastic base with circular blue glass frame, marked "Teletron," American.

Plate 36. Mantle or Shelf Clock, walnut case, Westminster chimes, English.

Plate 37. Mantle or Shelf Clock, walnut case, ebony trim, marked ''British-Made.''

Plate 38. Mantle Clock, 14½''l, 8¼''h, mahogany and walnut case with inlaid trim and numbers, German.

Plate 39. Mantle Clock, mahogany case, 13"h, 28"l, French, ca. 1920's.

Plate 40. Mantle or Shelf Clock, 10"l, 11½"h, ceramic, green glaze, chrome trim, figural dog painted gold, unmarked.

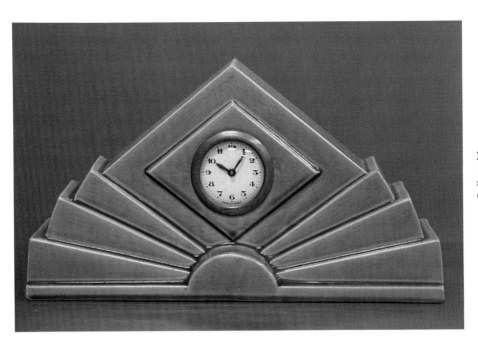

Plate 41. Mantle or Shelf Clock, 12"l, 7"h, ceramic, diamond and stepped fan shapes, marked "St. Clements, France," ca. 1925.

24

Dress Accessories

Style and fashion were an important part of the Deco era. Styles changed drastically for women, reflecting a more practical and carefree or casual attitude toward life. The clothing from the Deco years chronicles that transition. The long, corseted gowns of the late Victorian period changed to the knee length skirt and flat chested "boyish" look of the 1920's. Padded shoulders, tight skirts and baggy trousers followed in the late 1930's and 1940's. Although there were changes in men's clothing, styles remained conservative compared to the trends which came about with women's apparel.

Although time has been unkind to old garments, vintage Deco clothing is collectible, and there are dealers who specialize in fine examples salvaged from the period. Markets for this type of clothing are usually commercial or public, sold for store displays, museum exhibits or theatrical production rather than for individual use. But dresses, suits and coats made from the 1920's through the 1940's currently attract some of the teen and college age generations who enjoy actually wearing the outfits. Estate sales and thrift shops may yield some amusing examples at nominal prices.

While it may be difficult to find a piece of Deco clothing which one would care to wear, a number of items used to accessorize such clothing can be worn with enjoyment. Purses, compacts, belt buckles, dress clips and all types of jewelry are quite compatible with today's fashion. Dress accessories offer the collector an intriguing and almost unending source of Deco designs. It is apparent from the items shown, as is true for most surveys of the era, that dress accessories were primarily confined to women's articles. But cuff links, stickpins and watches, for example, were made in Deco styles for men.

Compacts are a product of the Deco age. These neat items made for checking or repairing one's make up, slipped easily into a purse or evening bag. While most contained a bit of mirror and a cake of powder, some were made with lipstick cases, change holders and money clips as well. The most expensive are made of gold and silver, but lower priced varieties made of plated or enamelled metals and celluloid or plastic are also available. Although small in size, compacts exhibit striking Deco traits. Notice the Egyptian influence on two examples, one with hierglyphics and one with Egyptian figures.

Mesh evening bags made from enamelled metals by American manufacturers such as Whiting and Davis were in demand during the 1920's. Small beaded and fringed bags were also popular accessories for the jazz age costume. Evening bags have become a special topic of collector interest and there are few bargains to be found. It is difficult to find one for less than $50. Large beaded purses, like the one illustrated, made during the latter part of the era do not cost nearly as much.

Collections of compacts and evening bags can be framed or housed in glass cases to add attractive touches to a room. The same can also be done for much less money with buttons or belt and shoe buckles. These little adornments are sometimes overlooked, but they often created the Deco accent for a garment. Such pieces usually outlived the clothing and many have been saved. Rummage through a box of old buttons and buckles, a Deco souvenir may be found—even a pair of fancy garters!

Jewelry is undoubtedly the most fascinating of all dress accessories. Although gold, silver and precious stones were fashioned into Deco designs, costume jewelry was born and thrived during those years. Many pieces were made from glass, enamelled metals, bakelite, celluloid and plastic. Rhinestones, like other good pieces of Deco costume jewelry, are attracting wide interest today. It is obvious that Deco designs have had a great influence on contemporary costume pieces. Reproductions also are surfacing on antique and collectible markets. Buyers should inspect jewelry carefully to determine if an item is new. Prices for authentic "period" pieces are often comparable with those of good quality modern costume jewelry. (For an excellent study of Art Deco jewelry, see Lillian Baker's *Art Nouveau and Art Deco Jewelry*.)

Plate 42. Compact, German silver, patented 1925. The transition from Art Nouveau is visible in the square "Deco" shape and "sunburst" ribbing combined with the "Nouveau" mythical "winged" images and delicate floral decor.

Plate 43. Compact, silver plated, "1929" engraved on front.

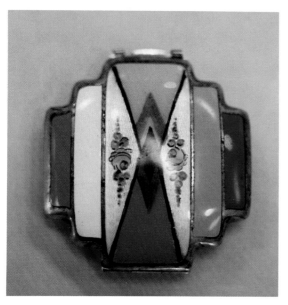

Plate 44. Compact, multi-colored enamel decorated with roses, brass plated trim.

Plate 45. Compact, navy plastic decorated with handpainted silver bar and wave lines, marked "France."

Plate 46. Compact in original box (Richard Hudnut, New York, Paris printed in top), silver case decorated with black and white enamel.

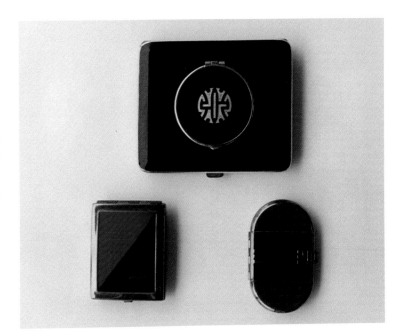

Plate 47. Group of Compacts: top, silver case covered with black enamel, gold hierglyphics in center; left, black and red enamel in a juxtaposed design, French; right, gold plated case with black enamelled bands, marked "Distributed by Lucien Lelong, New York-Chicago."

Plate 48. Compact, octagonal shape, brass plated, decorated with silver and black tangential designs on green enamel, marked "Richard Hudnut."

Plate 49. Compact, yellow and black enamel, Egyptian figural decor shows the King Tut influence, French.

Plate 50. Compact, gold painted, fitted with lipstick case. The compact slips into a black file carrying case (not shown), marked "Elgin, U. S. A."

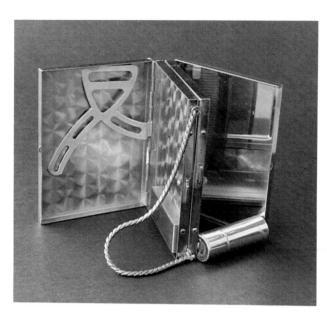

Plate 51. Compact, gold plated, fitted with lipstick case (left), money clip (right) and chain.

Plate 52. Belt Buckle, repetitive half-moon or crescent enamelled designs in shades of green, gold trim, German.

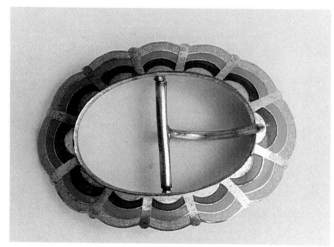

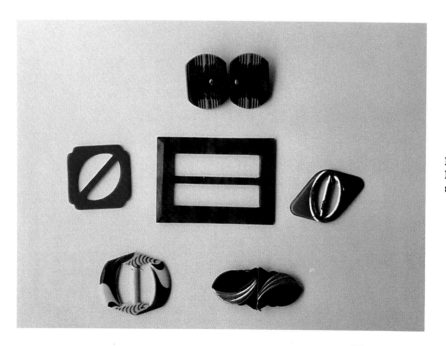

Plate 53. Belt Buckles representing a variety of Deco shapes. The center one is made of tortoise shell and the others are plastic.

Plate 54. Belt Buckle, multi-colored bakelite.

Plate 55. Watch pendant, 1¼"l, pentagon shape, green and black enamel, sterling silver trim, back (not shown) has vertical band of stylized flowers, marked "Borel."

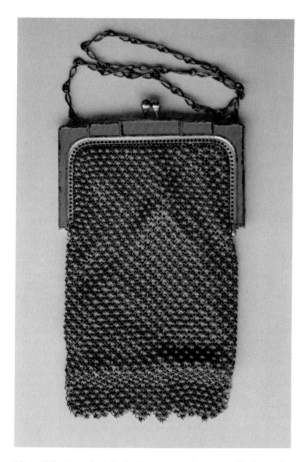

Plate 56. Evening Bag, deep orange enamelled mesh, made by Whiting and Davis, New York, ca. early 1920's.

Plate 57. Handbag, large white plastic beads fashioned in pentagon shape.

Plate 58. Beaded Garters, pink and white beads with butterfly wings.

Plate 59. Bracelet, black plastic, set with two large rhinestones.

Plate 60. Bracelet, red Czechoslovakian crystals and rhinestones, gold wash.

Plate 61. Pin and Earrings, 14K gold, black enamel, pin studded with small diamond.

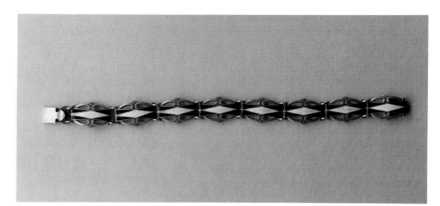

Plate 62. Bracelet, sterling silver, black and green enamelled work set in elongated diamond shapes, ca. 1920's.

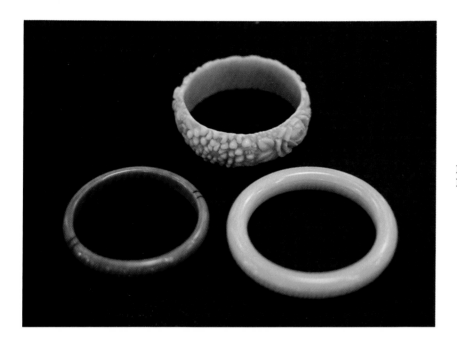

Plate 63. Group of three bakelite Bracelets.

Plate 64. Rhinestone Dress Clips, pavé settings in three different Deco designs.

31

Plate 65. Dress Clips: left, blue rhinestones and turquoise beads; right, multi-colored rhinestones.

Plate 66. Ear Clip and Brooch set fashioned of multi-colored rhinestones in abstract geometric form.

Plate 67. Matching Necklace, Bracelet and Ring, 14K white gold filagree combined with crystals cut with intaglio "rays," small diamond studs center of each piece.

Plate 68. Necklace, rhinestones set in large "V" shape, sterling silver chain.

Plate 69. Necklaces and Bracelet made of bakelite. The small necklace (top) and bracelet are trimmed with silver beads.

Plate 70. Necklace, orange and clear plastic cubes alternating with black beads.

Plate 71. Pin, large round and rectangular rhinestones set in square design.

33

Plate 72. Rhinestone Necklace with cascade shaped pendant.

Plate 73. Top, Rhinestone Bracelet, double row of alternating rectangular and circular stones; left, pin, gold cupid with stylized rhinestone wings; right, rhinestone pin, overlapping geometric shapes with pavé set stones frame large round stones, Eisenberg creations, ca. 1920's.

Plate 74. Pin, sterling silver 3"l, figural "tennis player," exhibiting "bobbed" hair and short skirt costume.

Plate 75. Pin, bakelite, abstract design.

Plate 76. Pin, large square cut blue glass stones and gold plated metal fashioned into stylized floral design.

Plate 77. Pin, elliptical green stone set in black and turquoise enamel, silver trim.

Plate 78. Pin, large amber glass stones studded with round crystals.

Dresser Accessories

Assorted grooming tools can be grouped under the category of dresser accessories simply because the dressing table or vanity is where they were usually kept. This category offers not only variety but also a plentiful supply of Art Deco collectibles. Like dress accessories, men's dresser items are few in number compared to women's. Comb and brush sets, cuff link boxes and shaving mugs may be found, however.

During Victorian times, the dresser "set" was in vogue. A set basically consisted of a tray with a matching powder box and hair receiver. Other pieces such as a "patch" box, pin box, ring tree, talcum shaker and even a chamber stick were sometimes included. The sets were usually made of porcelain, glass or silver. Their popularity carried over into the Deco era, although ring trees and hair receivers seem to have diminished popularity during the latter years.

Shapes and decoration of dresser sets gradually began to reflect the changing trends in designs. The floral and fanciful Art Nouveau decor of the late 1890's gave way to streamlined and geometric stylized designs in glass and silver. Porcelain sets began to have more vivid handpainted decoration, often with sharply contrasting colors. Deco dresser sets were also made in celluloid, or French ivory, as it was sometimes called. Hand mirrors, manicure tools and even perfume bottles were made to complement the celluloid sets.

Powder boxes, which might also double as small trinket boxes, are the most collectible items from the complete dresser sets. While it may be difficult to find all the matching pieces of an original set, surviving boxes are quite numerous. They were made in so many different sizes and with such diverse decorations that the search for a "different" one does not become boring. Collections can be easily and attractively displayed. Some of the boxes made during the Deco years were decorated with a nude or semi-nude figure on the lid. Others were even shaped as a figural box as shown in one example here. Powder boxes, like figural bookends, offer an opportunity to acquire a Deco figure for considerably less than a statue or figurine.

Other dresser accessories include combs, clothes brushes, hair brushes, jewelry boxes and perfume bottles. Collector interest in perfume bottles rivals or surpasses interest in powder boxes. Some of the famous European glass manufacturers of the period such as Lalique, Baccarat and Moser designed bottles with sharp Deco styles for perfumes and colognes made by various cosmetic firms. Today those original bottles are quite expensive, but others made by American glass companies, often unmarked and thus not attributable to a certain firm, are affordable. Even colognes sold in dime stores at the time which were bottled in Deco style containers or in dark blue, green or red glass are snapped up by collectors today.

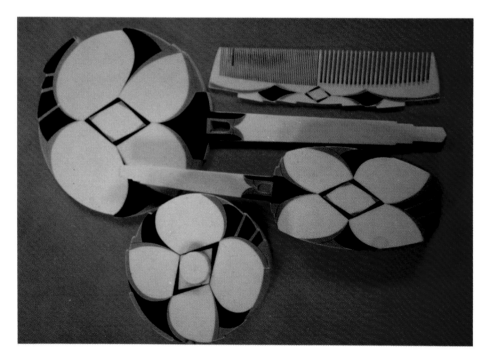

Plate 79. Matching Hand Mirror, Comb, Hair Brush and Powder box, celluloid with black and grey geometric designs and stylized floral decoration.

Plate 80. Man's Brush and Comb Set in
fitted case, monogrammed, nickel silver.

Plate 81. Hair Brush, brown plastic,
stepped design.

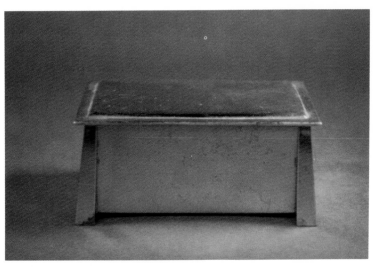

Plate 82. Jewel Box, 2½″h, 6½″l, nickel silver, interior lined with
black velvet.

Plate 83. Jewel Box, Limoges porcelain, octagonal shape, hand-painted abstract design, French.

Plate 84. Jewel Box, ceramic, black, green and yellow enamelled abstract designs, brass trim, 5½" x 4¼", marked "Boch Freres, Made in Belgium," artist signed, "A. Louviers."

Plate 85. Jewel Box, 8" x 5", brass, painted red and black with lid cut to form geometric and checkered designs.

Plate 86. Wash Bowl, 12½" d, and matching Pitcher, 9¼" h, ceramic, "Rose Marie" pattern, handpainted black and rose geometric decor, made by Keller and Guerin pottery, French.

Plate 87. Dresser Set, porcelain, Limoges, France blanks with hand-painted American decoration, blue and gold geometric shapes outlined with red; Dresser Tray, 16″l, pierced "butterfly" handles.

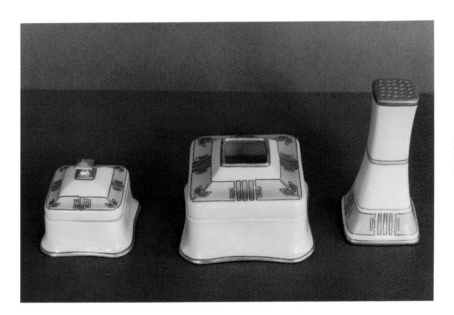

Plate 88. Matching pieces to Dresser Set: Pin Box, 2½″ sq., Hair Receiver, 4″ sq.; Talcum Shaker, 5″h.

Plate 89. Individual Perfume Bottles in gold fitted case, clear glass with gold plated tops, marked "Lucien Lelong."

Plate 90. Dresser Set, porcelain with silver and blue handpainted trim, Czechoslovakian; Candleholders, Powder Box and Pin Box.

Plate 91. Perfume Bottle, Black glass, silver lattice work border, French.

Plate 92. Perfume Bottle, 6½″ h, black glass decorated in gold with figures of a woman and child, French, designed by Iribe for Lanvin, ca. 1927.

Plate 93. Perfume Tray, 12″ x 9″, blue glass, chrome trim, center cameo of woman with dog painted in silver.

Plate 94. Perfume Bottle (left) and Powder Jar (right), 5¼″ h, amber glass, spherical bodies with cube shaped tops, signed "Moser," Karlsbad, Bohemia.

Plate 95. Powder Box, chrome with bakelite and ebony heart shapes on lid, glass insert, made by Chase.

Plate 96. Powder Box, 5½"h, chrome, decorated with three shades of green enamel, fitted with glass insert for powder, mirror inside lid.

Plate 97. Powder Box, 3½"d, ''Windsor Diamond'' pattern made by Jeanette Glass Company, ca. late 1930's.

Plate 98. Powder Box, ceramic, bold abstract decoration handpainted in vivid colors, black trim, artist signed, marked ''Made in Czechoslovakia.''

Plate 99. Powder Box, ceramic, decorated with dancing nude figure holding drape, German.

42

Plate 100. Powder box, 3½"h, 5"d, marble adorned with 5½"h enamelled pot metal figure in huntress attire, ivory face, unmarked.

Plate 101. Powder Box, 8½"h, frosted glass, semi-nude figural shape, unmarked.

Plate 102. Vanity Mirror on faux marble base with pot metal figure of nude posed in dance position.

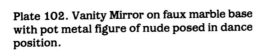

43

Lamps & Light Fixtures

Electricity was available to many American homes during the years between the First and Second World Wars. Electric lamps became an important part of the home furnishings market. Businesses such as department stores, offices, restaurants and theaters were another large sector of the economy in need of modern forms of light fixtures. Lighting manufacturers catered to both markets, parlaying topical Deco themes into various forms of light.

Floor lamps and table top lamps are both quite collectible. Selections may be elegant and high style or simply low camp and amusing. Lamps are not only ingenious relics of Deco design but they are also functional. Collectors should check the electrical wiring, however. Many still have the original cords which may be frayed or split, but rewiring is not too expensive. It is well worth the effort to have lamps repaired so that they can be displayed to full advantage. Rewiring does not detract but rather adds to the lamp's value.

Floor lamps supported widely flared shades or globes. These reflected the light upward and *torchere* has become the name associated with that particular style. The shades were made of frosted or opaque glass or out of metal such as brass or chrome. This same type of lamp is now frequently reproduced to complement new Deco style furniture. Other Deco floor lamps had conventional parchment or silk shades with the "modern" look showing up in the stems and bases.

Figural table lamps are very much in demand. Both French and American companies made numerous varities aimed at the middle class market. Women, nude or semi-nude, were fashioned in various stylized poses such as dancing, kneeling or with arms stretched high in the air. The light globe was positioned to the side or behind the figure or even rested in the figure's hands. These lamps were decorative objects, designed to cleverly disguise the source of light.

Although this type of figural lamp was made in bronze, most of the ones found today were made of metal alloys. The finish may be bronze colored or painted red, black, green and so forth. Because the paint wears and chips over time, it is not uncommon for the lamps to be repainted, especially for resale. But lower prices should be reflected if that is the case, Globes on these lamps, because of their fragile nature, often have been replaced as well. It goes without saying that the most desirable lamps are those with all original parts and finish.

Regarding prices, the French figural lamps are the most expensive, and it is not uncommon for these to cost $1,000 or more, outsided the range for the moderate collector. While American specimens are considerably

less costly, it is still rare to find an all original one for less than $100. Those not in working order and needing repairs are about the only ones which might be bargains. The Frankart Company, located in New York City, was probably the most prolific manufacturer of metal figural Deco items. Frankart lamps, like their other products, have become increasingly popular. Consequently, prices continue to rise, ranging from $200 to $600.

Ceramic and glass Deco lamps were also made in figural designs. One ceramic lamp shown here, made by Van Briggle, is a finely executed piece of American art pottery. The boudoir lamp with the nude glass globe is a mass produced piece imitating the Lalique style. Other ceramic lamps portray a Deco influence by their hand-painted body decor in geometric or stylized configurations. Glass lamps may feature similar Deco characteristics in either the body or the shade as illustrated in some of the photographs.

Deco light fixtures designed for commercial enterprises can be turned into attractive lighting for homes. *Torchere* or conical shaped wall sconces adapt to baths, halls and bedrooms while cascading chandeliers and other large fixtures can be used to light entrance foyers or porches. Shops specializing in architectural antiques may offer some interesting examples. Most commercial fixtures were made of bronze, brass or even cast iron, and these have survived the years quite well. Shapes are unquestionably Deco!

Plate 103. Boudoir Lamp, 8½"l, 8"h, pot metal, painted green finish, seated nude figure, amber crackle glass globe, American, marked "Kelly Creations."

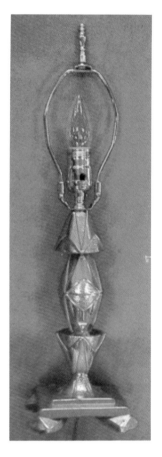

Plate 104. Table lamp, marked ''1928, Armour Bronze Corp,'' metal alloy with lacquered copper finish, combination of different geometric shapes stacked on footed stepped base.

Plate 105. Table Lamp, brass, slag glass panels and silk fringe enhance octagonal shaped shade.

Plate 106. Boudoir Lamp, dancing nude figure, pot metal with bronze finish, marked ''Rhythm'' on base, 8½" h. When the bulb is turned on behind the splotched painted glass shade, there is an illusion of movement.

Plate 107. Boudoir Lamp, 8" h, pot metal base incorporates Art Nouveau lines. Frosted glass shade exhibits Deco style with nude figure and molded overlapping half moon designs on corners.

Plate 108. Table Lamp, ceramic, figural nude base, blue matt glaze, marked ''Van Briggle,'' Colorado Springs Art Pottery.

Plate 109. Table Lamp, 19½"h, porcelain figure dressed in long gown, elaborate headdress supports the shade, a sphere made of slag glass, burled wood base, Cubist influence, marked ''Argilor, Paris.''

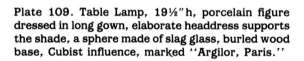

Plate 110. Pair of Boudoir or Vanity Lamps, white metal, bronze colored finish, nudes in stylized positions, marked ''Frankart.''

Plate 111. Lamp, 21"h, semi-nude figure, white metal with silver finish, black marble base. The tambourine serves as light shade, marked ''Fayral,'' French, ca. mid 1920's.

47

Plate 112. Boudoir Lamp, pot metal, painted green finish, dancing nude figure, marked "Beaver patent pending," American. (Shade is not original.)

Plate 113. Table Lamp, 11½"h, glass, represents the planet Saturn, commemorative of the 1939 World's Fair.

Plate 114. Table Lamp, 14"h, cascade or waterfall shaped shade, opalescent glass marked "Sabino," French.

Plate 115. Wall Sconce, brass, 10″ h, typical fixture for theaters, American.

Plate 116. Sconce, painted metal, frosted glass shade with interior painted pink, American.

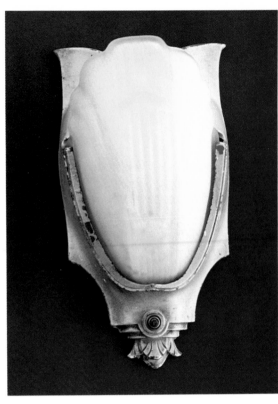

Plate 117. Wall Sconce, 14½″ h, chrome, French.

Plate 118. Commercial Light Fixture, 29½″ h, copper and bronze with opaline glass panels.

Library & Study Accessories

Numerous types of items associated with reading and writing were made along Deco lines. Bookends, ink wells and desk sets are representative items. Such accessories are expected to be found in a library or study setting and complement its furnishings. These often have a bold or masculine look as well as Deco traits. Additional objects have been included in this category. These could easily be found in the library although one might find them in other rooms as well. For example, radios, electric fans and wallhangings are shown in this section.

Desk accessories made nice gifts, and it is not unusual to find monograms on such items as letter openers and desk boxes. Most of the sets were made of metal, usually brass, bronze or silver. Fine jewelry and department stores had desk items made especially for their firms. The company name appeared either alone or with the manufacturer's name on pieces. Expect pieces with such famous names as Cartier or Tiffany to be quite expensive. Desk items made and marked by American metal companies such as Silvercrest, Bronz-Met and Heintz are usually moderately priced.

Figural bookends are an interesting Deco library accessory. As is the case with most figural pieces, the bookends say "Deco" at a glance. These seem to be the least expensive of any type of figural pieces as indicated by the prices quoted for examples shown here. Figures made into bookends do not require the same amount of workmanship that some other figural combinations do, such as clocks or lamps. Moreover, some of these are two dimensional and stamped from a metal sheet. Collectors searching for an affordable Deco figure will find that bookends offer some good possibilities.

Plate 119. Bookends, nudes in dance position, bronze with green finish, stylized floral design on base, 5"h, marked "Schroedin, Solid Bronze."

Plate 120. Magazine Rack, 15½″h, 11″d, nude and frolicking greyhound, bronze with silver finish.

Plate 121. Bookends, nudes with arms stretch overhead, male kneeling at feet, 8″h, marked with ''Bronzmet'' insignia and ''Pat. July 22, 1924, copyright 1923, Gifthouse, Inc. NYC.''

Plate 122. Bookends, bronze, 8″h, nudes flanked by pair of greyhound. The curvilinear arch work enhances the streamlined figures, German, ca. early 1920's.

Plate 123. Three brass Door Knockers, 6½″l, Egyptian influence. Such items are often used for Paperweights.

53

Plate 124. Bookend, 6½"h, black, rose and white marble combined in geometric configuration.

Plate 125. Newspaper Holder, 11¼"h, 8½"w, metal, copper finish.

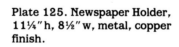

Plate 126. Bookends, Scottie Dogs, 7"h, metal, brass finish, made by Frankart.

Plate 127. Bookends, Sailboats, 7"h, made by Bronze Art.

Plate 128. Inkwell and Pen Tray, sterling silver decoration on bronze, made by the Heintz Art Metal Company, Buffalo, New York.

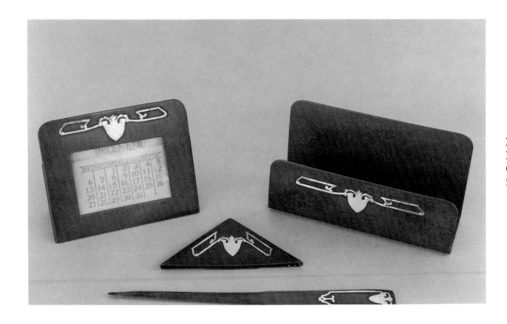

Plate 129. Calendar Holder, Envelope Holder, Blotter Corner and Letter Opener matching Inkwell and Pen Tray in preceding photograph.

Plate 130. Desk Accessories: Calendar and Envelope Holders, bronze, marked "Silvercrest," American.

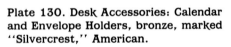

Plate 131. Inkwell, bronze with silver finish, 2¼" h, black marble base, 6¼" x 4½", signed "Rischmann," French.

56

Plate 132. Inkwell, hammered copper and cast brass.

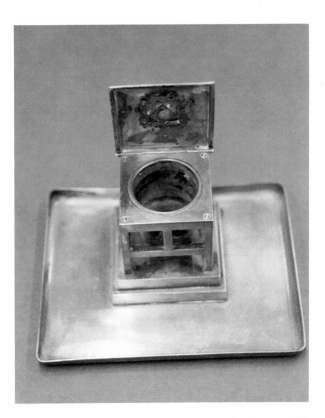

Plate 133. Inkwell, brass, 3½"h, attached tray, 6"l.

Plate 134. Picture Frame, beveled glass, etched floral and leaf designs, 14½" x 17", ca. 1940's.

Plate 135. Picture Frame, 6" x 8", brass.

Plate 136. Picture Frame, wood and glass. The picture illustrates a suite of bedroom furniture designed by Andre Domin for the 1925 Paris Exhibition.

Plate 137. Temperature Gauge, plastic, 3½" sq., marked "Taylor Humidiguide."

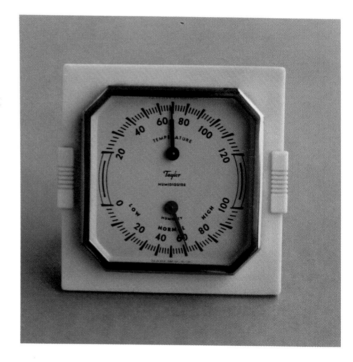

Plate 138. Ceiling Fan made in the form of an airplane engine and propeller (chrome). Mounted in a ceiling which explains the extraordinary angle of the picture.

Plate 139. Oscillating Electric Fan, 12″d, marked "Gilbert," brass blades.

Plate 140. Radio, 17″l, 9″h, blue glass and wood, chrome trim, marked "Spartan."

Plate 141. Radio, 8″ x 11″, wood and chrome, marked "Fada."

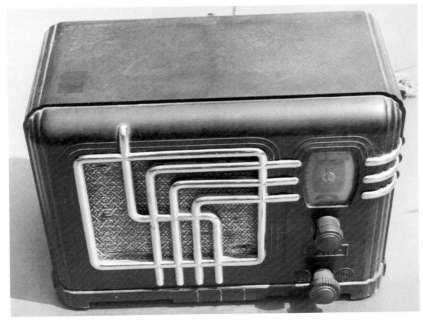

Plate 142. Tapestry, Egyptian figures and hieroglyphics.

Plate 143. Tapestry, 64½"l, Egyptian motif featuring a Sphinx, French.

Plate 144. Wrought Iron Grate, 38½" x 23½", abstract geometric and floral designs, marked "Made in France."

Smoking Accessories

The cigarette, like the cocktail, became a mark of sophistication, one of the "in" things during the Deco years. To smoke (and drink) showed one was in step with the "modern" world. This was especially true for women as they shed the forbidding Victorian rules dictating "proper" conduct. More and more women began to smoke in public just as they shortened their hemlines and bobbed their hair.

A number of interesting smoker's items were made which were either desirable or necessary accessories for those addicted to the habit. For example, ashtrays were indispensable. Both table top and free standing varieties became common fixtures in the home. Most were made of metals such as brass, copper, bronze and chrome but glass and ceramic ones were also prevalent. The ever popular nude figures sometimes were incorporated into the design. Two shown here include a rather simple table top model and an elaborate floor style.

In conjunction with ashtrays, "silent butlers" became an appropriate household item. The name was an apt description for this receptacle fitted with a long handle and hinged lid. For those who had no real butler, these were handy gadgets for emptying overflowing ashtrays at one's party or cleaning up the stale remains the next day! They were usually made of chrome, brass or frequently hammered aluminum. The latter type, however, do not always fit the Deco image even though they are from the period.

Cigarette holders cover a broad category of smoking collectibles. In fact, the term "holder" can have several different meanings when used in connection with cigarettes. Table top holders refer to open or covered boxes for keeping a convenient supply of cigarettes. These were made as individual containers or as a combination piece with space for cigarettes and matches and even an ashtray. The boxes were also often part of a matching set of separate pieces.

Another type of holder was the cigarette dispenser. These are novel items and a good example of the "purely fun" side of the Deco years. One of the dispensers shown is a "pop-up" type, operating with a spring device. Cigarettes encased in metal holders pop up when the lid is removed. Another has concealed push buttons on two sides. When pressed, the hinged lid opens, revealing individual spaces for cigarettes. A third type of dispenser has a roll-top. When it is pushed back, a tray slides out offering five cigarettes.

The term cigarette holder, however, is perhaps most commonly associated with the individual holder. While these were designed for keeping the cigarette from direct contact with the mouth, they were also used for effect, to impact a chic or debonair look! The holders shown here range in length from two to six inches. They are made of plastic, tortoise shell or celluloid.

Art Deco cigarette lighters comprise still another group of smoking accessories. Collectors are interested in both the table top and the pocket or purse varieties. Most of the pocket lighters have masculine overtones. Of course, it was the custom for a man to light a woman's cigarette. Two lighters shown here with floral decor appear strictly feminine, however. One, in fact, is a combination compact and cigarette lighter.

The "bar-tender" lighter is probably the most coveted of the table top models among Deco enthusiasts. Several variations of the type featured here were made by different companies such as Ronson and the Art Metal Works. Some functioned as a cigarette dispenser as well as a lighter. Although they were made as novelties, these rather scarce items fetch hundreds of dollars today.

Incense burners are included in this section. They may be used to mask tobacco odors, and they are complementary in a decorative scheme. Other tobacco related Deco collectibles include cigarette and cigar cases, cigar clippers and cutters, pipe stands, tobacco jars and humidors. Beware that general collectors of tobacciana make the market quite competitive.

Plate 145. Ashtray, floor model, nude figure, 24"h, arms stretched overhead to support tray, cast metal, made by Frankart.

Plate 147. Ashtray, ceramic, 4"d, marked "Snufferette, National Porcelain Co., Trenton, N. J."

Plate 146. Ashtray, 5"d, blue glass decorated with chrome sailboat, marked "F. D. Co.," American.

Plate 148. Ashtray, ceramic, cobalt blue glaze, 4½"d, marked "Snufferette, Ekstrand Mfg. Co., Inc., NY, The Executive."

Plate 149. Ashtray, seated nude figure, cast metal, painted gold finish, amber glass tray, marked "Nu Art," made by Imperial Glass Company, Ohio.

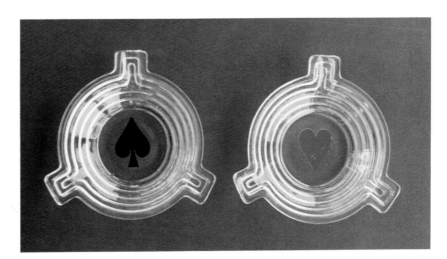

Plate 150. Ashtrays, 4"d, "Manhattan" pattern Depression Glass decorated with suits of playing cards, made by Anchor Hocking Glass Co. of Ohio.

Plate 151. Assortment of black glass ashtrays in several geometric styles, unmarked.

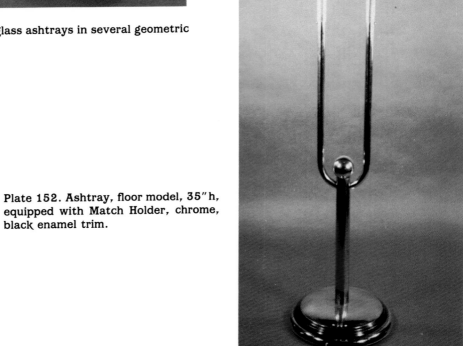

Plate 152. Ashtray, floor model, 35"h, equipped with Match Holder, chrome, black enamel trim.

Plate 153. Ashtray, floor model, 33″h, cast metal, silver finish, stepped designed handle and tray (glass insert), marked ''Seville Art Studio.''

Plate 154. This ashtray and the following three photographs are examples of smoking accessories made by the Heintz Art Metal Company. They are marked with the Heintz monogram and ''Sterling on Bronze,'' patent date 1912. This ashtray was part of a nested set made for the B. Altman Company. The Heintz pieces all have various stylized geometric designs in sterling silver.

Plate 155. Smoking Set: left, Match Holder; center, Tray, 10″d with Ashtray and book Match Holder; right, Cigarette Holder.

Plate 156. Cigarette and Match Holder combination, 2½″h, 6″l.

Plate 157. Smoking Set: Ashtray, Cigarette Holder, Match Holder, Indian symbol motif.

Plate 158. Ashtray, 7″l, chrome with black enamel trim.

Plate 159. Ashtray, ceramic, 6"l, woman's profile fitted with bathing cap, handpainted, Japanese.

Plate 160. Ashtray, 5½"l, chrome.

Plate 161. Ashtrays, chrome: left, 4½"d, figural bird beaks hold cigarette, marked "Diecasters, Ridgefield, N. J."; right, 4"d, unmarked.

Plate 162. Silent Butler, 11½"l, chrome with bakelite handle, marked "Chase."

Plate 163. Silent Butler, 9"l, chrome, unmarked.

Plate 164. Cigarette Holder, 2½"h, open sphere on square pedestal base, marked "Chase."

Plate 165. Cigarette Box, seated nude figure, white metal, silver finish. The figure is marked "W. B. Mfg. Co." The glass box is the "Ridgeleigh" pattern made by the A.H. Heisey Glass Co., Newark, Ohio.

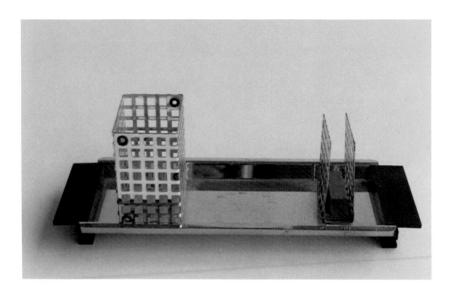

Plate 166. Cigarette and Book Match Holder combination, 9"l, chrome and black plastic, unmarked.

Plate 167. Cigarette Box, 5½"l, 5"h, black and red plastic.

Plate 168. Match Holder, 4"h, attached tray, brass.

Plate 169. Cigarette Dispenser, 6¼"h, black enamel and chrome. This device opens with a pull spring top. The cigarettes are held by individual metal holders.

Plate 170. Cigarette Dispenser, 3"h, silverplate, French. The top springs open when the small triangular shapes on either side are pressed.

Plate 171. Cigarette Dispenser, 4½"h, wedge shaped, burled maple wood. The top of the wedge slides up to reveal the cigarettes.

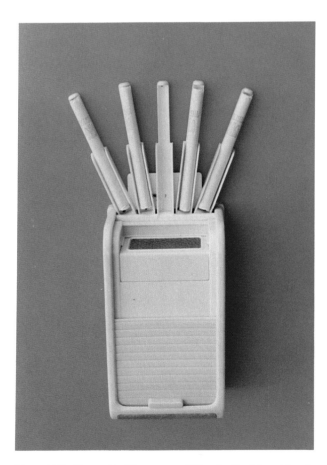

Plate 172. Cigarette Dispenser, 6"l, plastic. The cigarettes roll out of the case by sliding back the lid, marked ''Ziegfield.''

Plate 173. Cigarette Dispenser, 5"h, 7½"l, wood, painted red exterior and black interior. The box has a stepped shape when closed.

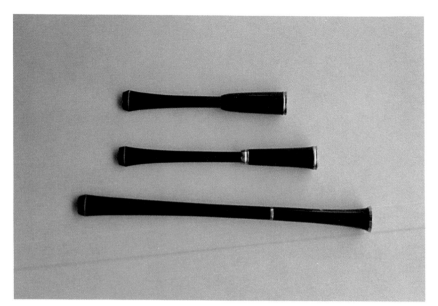

Plate 174. Individual Cigarette Holders, black plastic trimmed with narrow gold bands: 5″l; 3″l; 2½″l.

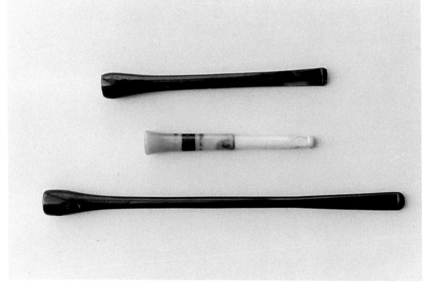

Plate 175. Individual Cigarette Holders: black plastic, 6″l; celluloid, 3″l; tortoise shell, 4″l.

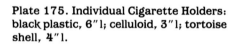

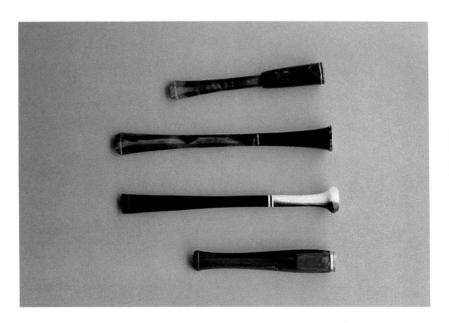

Plate 176. Individual Cigarette Holders: blue plastic and tortoise shell, 2½″l; black plastic and tortoise shell, 3½″l; black and white plastic, marbled effect, 3½″l; blue plastic, silver trim, 2″l.

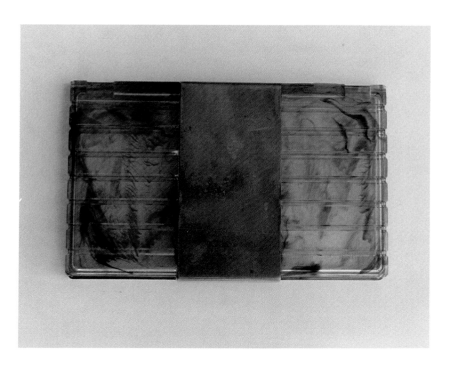

Plate 177. Cigarette Case, bakelite and pigskin, sliding top, marked "A. Rolinx, Made in England."

Plate 178. Pocket Lighters: tortoise shell, marked "Ronson, Pat. Nov. 19-23"; white enamel, chrome rainbow designs, marked "Evan"; red and black enamel, chrome trim, floral decor combined with stepped designs, marked "Evan."

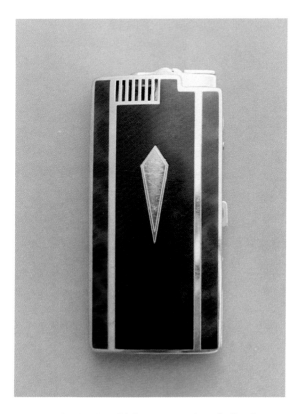

Plate 179. Pocket Lighter, tortoise shell, chrome trim, made by Ronson.

Plate 180. Pocket and Purse Lighters: gold plated, rocket design on checkerboard background, marked "Royal"; combination lighter and compact, white enamel, gold trim, pink roses, marked "Marathon, Made in U. S. A."

Plate 181. Table model Cigarette Lighter, "Bar-Tender" type made by the Art Metal Works of Newark, NJ, chrome and painted metal, 5½″ h, 8″ l.

Plate 182. Reverse view of "Bar-Tender" Lighter.

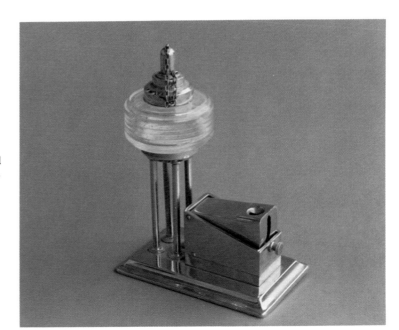

Plate 183. Table model Cigar lighter with fuel reservoir, and Clipper, chrome and glass, unmarked.

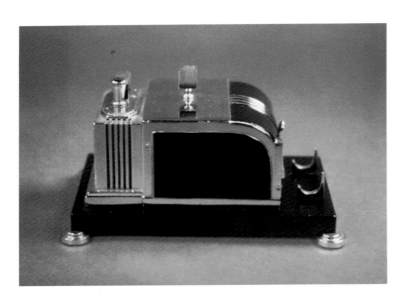

Plate 184. Cigarette Lighter and Dispenser, black enamel and chrome 8″l, 4″h, made by Ronson. Cigarettes roll out by sliding back the lid on the right side.

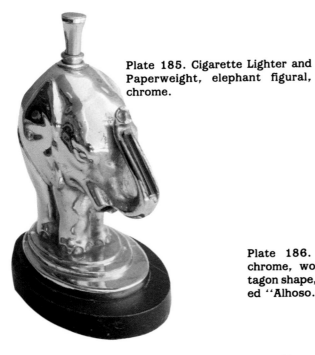

Plate 185. Cigarette Lighter and Paperweight, elephant figural, chrome.

Plate 186. Cigar Clipper, chrome, wooden base, octagon shape, German, marked ''Alhoso.''

Plate 187. Pipe Stand, bronze, nude figure poised in diving position, unmarked.

Plate 188. Humidor, 7¼"h, bronze, sterling silver decor, monogrammed and dated "4-4-23," made by the Heintz Art Metal Company.

Plate 189. Incense Burner, ceramic, 6½"h, figural, Egyptian dress, artist signed, "Lisne," French.

Plate 190. Incense Burner, bronze figure, Egyptian influence, signed "L. V. Aronson," ca. early 1920's.

Plate 191. Incense Burner, 6½"h, cast iron, floral designs combined with geometric form, marked "Made in France."

Plate 192. Incense Burner, cast metal figure, black finish, Egyptian motif, marked "Vantiens, Made in France."

Statues

Figures, more than any other category of decorative accessory, seem to say "Deco" best. The statues exhibit not only features commonly associated with Art Deco, but also they express the spirit of freedom and optimism in the future that prevailed at the time. It is not surprising that these personifications beguile collectors. As noted earlier, figures were so popular that they were fashioned into dual purpose articles as well as art objects. This section, however, contains only the latter. Statues, statuettes or figurines and a few head forms or busts are included. (For additional examples of figures, see Ashtrays, Bookends, Candle Holders, Incense Burners and Lamps.)

Most of the Deco figural subjects were women. Pieces were made with couples forming dance partners or duets. Men were also modeled as sportsmen or represented as mythical gods or even circus clowns. Animals made along Deco lines are not so rare as male examples but they are less prevalent than female themes. All kinds of animals, however, were made as decorative sculpture. Members of the cat family (jaguar, panther, tiger) and deer, elk and gazelles as well as dogs (like the greyhound) projected the essential components of the Deco image—speed, grace and sleekness. Certain animals, especially dogs, were often part of female dominated scenes. Even birds such as cockatoos, ducks, parrots and penquins were shaped in stylized forms to fit in with "modern" decor.

The nude or semi-nude female apparently was the most favorite figural topic of the period. It is held in no less esteem by collectors. Poses varied from lanquid, reclining positions to ones expressing movement. Grace and speed were implied by various dance positions or hair shaped as wings or fashioned in a "wind blown" style. Kneeling or standing figures with arms stretched forward symbolized movement into the future. Arms stretched overhead, perhaps holding a globe or sphere, seem to indicate awareness and interest in the world at large.

While the nude and semi-nude figures may suggest the spirit of the period, fully clothed models portray the dress and hair styles in vogue. Interest in other cultures was also exhibited by the figure's costume. The Egyptian influence was dominant in the mid 1920's, after the opening of King Tut's tomb in 1923. Several of the figures shown in this section and some in other categories (see Lamps and Incense Burners) flaunt the trappings of Egyptian attire such as metal breastplates, harem pants and elaborate headdresses. Female figures with black finishes show the influence of African art and black American entertainers. Jazz musicians and torch singers became very popular during the 1920's, especially in France.

Decorative figures not only were made in a number of sizes and poses, but also they were made from many different materials, including bronze, copper, metal alloys, plaster, pottery and porcelain. The French bronzes are the most coveted and most expensive. Bronze combined with ivory and precious jewels, silver or gold is called "chryselephantine" work. D.H. Chiparus, who worked in France, is noted to have excelled in this type of sculpture. Prices for his original pieces are in the tens of thousands of dollars today. Collectors should be aware, however, that current bronze manufacturers reproduce or imitate some of his figures as well as several other famous sculptors of the period. Although advertised as manufactured with the "lost wax" method and sporting the same or similarly spelled names of well known artists such as Chiparus, Zach or Preiss, these bronzes are still only replicas and not from the period. Unfortunately, they are sometimes sold by dealers as authentic sculptures. Wholesale prices are not cheap, but do not be surprised to find that sum multiplied several times over when such an item is sold in a retail outlet.

Because bronzes were expensive to manufacture, it did not take entrepreuers long to recognize the value of mass producing similar statues from metal alloys. Pot metal, white metal or spelter are names frequently used to identify such alloys. Psuedo bronze figures were made in both Europe and America. Even if a piece can be identified as being of French origin, do not assume the metal is bronze. Many of the pot metal pieces were executed quite well. Different patinations and finishes were used to give either a "bronze" look or colored surface. Some were even made with ivory faces and hands, imitating chryselephatine types. Fabricated ivory, often called "ivorene," was sometimes used, however.

Patination and cold painted are two terms used to describe bronze finishes. Patination refers to a colored finish which is fired onto the metal and thus becomes permanent. Cold painted means the finish was not fired onto the metal. Lacquer was applied to preserve the color, but this type of finish is not totally permanent. Some of the metal alloy figures were simply painted without any sealing coat. Consequently, over time, the paint has chipped or become noticeably worn. Those with apparent surface damage can sometimes be purchased for bargain prices. Dealers have them repainted, but prices should not be the same as for those in good or original condition. Inspect figures carefully for detail to note signs of age and wear on finished as well as whether there are chips on the face, hair or limbs.

Because of the demand for Deco figures, pot metal

statues are far from cheap. Those in good condition, depending on size, will cost several hundred dollars. It is not uncommon for examples to cost $1,000 or more, especially if it can be determined the piece was made in France. It is rare to find any authentic Deco metal figure for less than $100.

Porcelain figurines were made by several European factories prior to World War II. Goldscheider, an Austrian company, is well known for its Deco pieces. Some of the firms who are more famous for their table wares also produced figural items during that time. The Lenox china company in Trenton, New Jersey, made porcelain figures which portrayed Deco themes. Porcelain pieces are generally much more moderately priced than metal statues, but they still are not cheap. Few cost less than $200.

Earthenware or simple pottery figures were also made in this country and abroad. Usually earthenware items are less expensive than those made of hard paste porcelain or bone china. Not only was the manufacturing process cheaper, but also earthenware is not as strong. It chips and breaks easily and also can become discolored or crazed over time. Pottery figures, however, are often comparable or higher in price than porcelain ones. Those made by American art potteries are very collectible. Some made by American companies, which produced inexpensive pottery dishes and accessories, also made a few figures. Such items were not the company's main product, and thus the figures are scarce, as well as popular, and bring high prices compared with other items they manufactured.

The statues and figurines are grouped here according to their composition: Ceramic (pottery and porcelain), Plaster and Metals (bronze, copper & metal alloys).

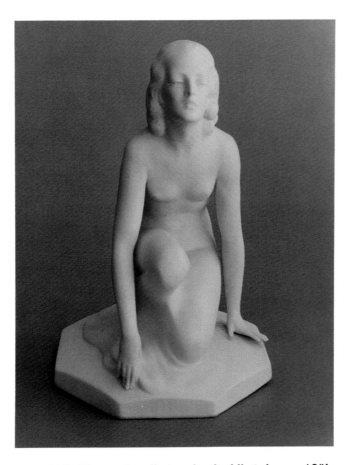

Plate 193. Figure, kneeling nude shedding drape, 10"h, porcelain, white matte finish, octagonal shaped base, German, signed "Poerzl," G. Greiner factory mark, ca. late 1920's. The artist was a noted German designer of metals and ceramics.

Plate 194. Madonna, 10″h, porcelain, artist signed, marked ''Goldscheider,'' Austrian, ca. early 1920's.

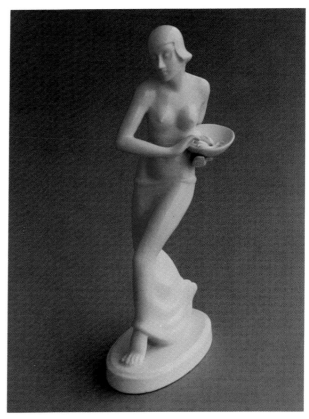

Plate 195. Semi-Nude Figure, 11"h, ceramic, Egyptian influence, marked "Kent Art Ware," Japanese.

Plate 196. Ceramic Figure modeled after Dorothy Lamour, film star famous for wearing a sarong. The statuette was made by Clark Pottery of East Palestine, Ohio, ca. 1940's.

Plate 197. Cinderella, 12″h, ceramic with high glaze finish, marked "Goldscheider." This figure was made after the Goldscheider factory relocated from Austria to America, ca. 1940's.

Plate 198. Clown playing accordion, ceramic, high glaze finish, 12"h, marked "Royal Dux," Czechoslovakian.

Plate 199. Dancer with fan, 12″h, porcelain, mounted on metal base, unmarked, attributed to Goldscheider.

Plate 201. Vanity Doll Head, 5½"h, ceramic, marked "G & K Keramik, Made in Austria."

Plate 200. Vanity Bust, ceramic, artist signed "Elly Strobach," marked "Royal Dux," Czechslovakian.

Plate 202. Nude Figure posed in dance position, ceramic, 8½"h, 11"l, made by the Camden Art and Tile Co., Camden, Arkansas.

Plate 203. Pair of ceramic Birds, high glaze green finish, signed "Ch. Lemanceau," French designer of pottery animals.

83

Plate 204. Tigers, porcelain, 9½"l overall, German, made by Hutchenreuther, ca. early 1920's.

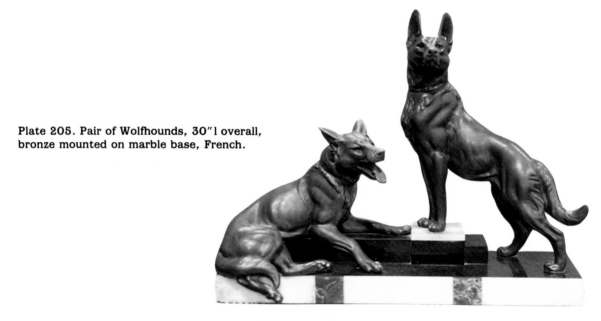

Plate 205. Pair of Wolfhounds, 30"l overall, bronze mounted on marble base, French.

Plate 206. Pair of Russian Wolfhounds, 13"l overall, ceramic, German, signed "B. Kopecki," ca. 1940's.

Plate 207. Reclining Woman in long gown posed with Greyhound, 25"l overall, plaster, marked "Pecchioli."

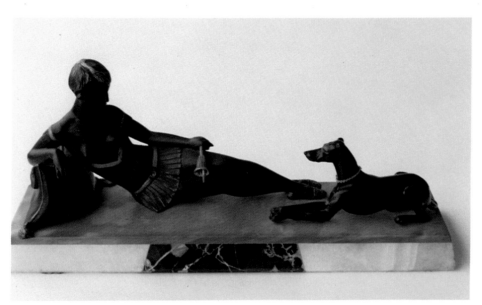

Plate 208. Semi-Nude Figure and canine posed in reclining position, pot metal, black matte finish, gold accents, mounted on marble base, 16½"l overall, marked "France."

Plate 209. Mannekin Head, 10"h, plaster, gold finish.

Plate 210. Woman modeled with Wolfhounds, 14"l, 12"h, faux marble, marked "A. Santini."

Plate 211. Chiparus type Figure, pot metal, red lacquered finish, ivory face, marble base, 7"h. (A similar figure is being reproduced today.)

Plate 212. Copper Figure, 14"h, bronze finish, Egyptian influence.

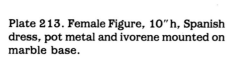

Plate 213. Female Figure, 10"h, Spanish dress, pot metal and ivorene mounted on marble base.

Plate 214. Semi-Nude Figure posed in dance position, 21"h overall, white metal, bronze finish, mounted on black marble base, marked "Fayral," French, ca. 1920's.

Table Wares

Companies engaged in manufacturing products for preparing and serving food found it necessary to accommodate the new trends in modern design. Streamlined and angular shapes can be found not only in sets of china but in kitchen equipment as well. In this section, table wares are not confined to dishes but include other utilitarian and decorative pieces. Because of the great diversity of this category, it is possible to show only a sample of items, but the pieces illustrated should alert collectors to the many possibilities table wares offer. Photographs are arranged approximately in alphabetical order according to the function of the item, ranging from candle holders, centerpieces and crumbers, to pitchers and a toaster!

Table wares basically are made of pottery, glass or metal. Ceramics include earthenware or semi-china, stoneware and porcelain. Simplified decoration distinguishes Deco china from that produced during the Victorian years. Floral transfer patterns covering the entire surface of china gave way to colored line borders or abstract geometric patterns. Sometimes china was left undecorated with the shape or mold drawing attention to a modern image. Geometric shapes other than the usual circular form are seen here in the rectangular bowl and the triangular shaped cup and saucer.

Ceramic table wares can be found at all price levels. Pieces designed and handpainted by Clarice Cliff for the Royal Staffordshire Pottery during the late 1920's and early 1930's are highly regarded by advanced collectors. Price can reach several hundred to several thousand dollars for some examples, especially those with floral and landscape decor. "Bizarre," "Geometric," and "Fantasque" were some of the pattern names. The English artist's signature was included on most of her work. Pieces which do not have her name or signature as part of the mark are usually considerably lower in price. "The Biarritz" soup bowl shown here is one such example. Although the pattern is quite simple, it also merits consideration as a form of Deco table ware. Deco patterns by other English potters are also quite collectible. Many good examples in the moderate price ranges are surfacing. These may be found mixed in with other miscellaneous dishes by dealers who do not specialize in Art Deco.

"American Modern," designed by Russel Wright for the Ohio based Steubenville Pottery is also quite collec-

tible and much lower in price. This line was made from about 1939 through the late 1950's. Solid colored surfaces without other added decoration implied a modern concept. Many other European and American pottery and porcelain factories produced their own renditions of "modern" style. Japanese table ware companies used similar interpretations to reach the large American market. Deco patterned china made by the Noritake firm has been attracting many collectors during the last few years. Prices are still affordable but not inconsequential. Table china, however, is probably the largest source of Art Deco "sleepers" and possible bargains today.

Angular shapes or stylized designs cut or molded into glass table wares were made to grace the dining tables of the period. Art glass by French manufacturers is usually too expensive for moderate collectors. The large blue centerpiece bowl made by Daum and the smoke glass bowl by Verlys are two such examples. These would fall into the "investment" rather than the "fun" class of Deco collectibles. But, like ceramics, many types of inexpensive table glass were made during the 1930's and 1940's by American factories. Depression era glass collectors began to salvage pieces during the 1960's. A number of the patterns have unmistakable Deco characteristics. "Manhattan," a clear glass pattern made by Anchor Hocking is just one type finding its way into Deco collections. The ruby red, cobalt blue and deep green colored glass made by other American glass companies also qualifies as Deco. Quite a few pieces are very attractive, some are even elegant and others are just amusing.

Flatware, serving pieces and decorative table articles can be found in silver, brass, copper, chrome and plated metals. Chrome and plated metals are the least expensive. Nude or semi-nude figures were made into metal centerpieces or candle holders. Prices are competitive with other figural items and examples are just as much in demand. A number of metal Deco items were originally silverplated. Because the plating wears off, items become ugly and lose much of their value. Dealers have found it lucrative to have such objects stripped to the base metal which was usually copper or brass. The copper centerpiece with a pot metal nude is an example which was once silver plated. Do not automatically disregard badly worn plated pieces which have obvious Deco signs. It may be wise to have them stripped and polished by a commercial firm which specializes in that kind of work.

Plate 215. Candle Holder, 15″h, two light, pot metal figure, silver finish, mounted on mahogany stand, English.

Plate 216. Candle Holder, 6″h, porcelain, stylized birds and geometric patterns, handpainted, Japanese, made by Noritake.

Plate 217. Candle Holder, 4″h, "Tuscany" pattern made by the Roseville Pottery.

Plate 218. Candle Holder, 7″ h, glass, sharp angular shape, unmarked.

Plate 219. Candle Holders, 6½″ h, glass etched base, made by New Martinsville Glass Company, New Martinsville, Virginia.

Plate 220. Candle Holders, frosted blue glass, 5½″ h, sailboat theme.

Plate 221. Candle Holders, 5″h, sterling on bronze made by the Heintz Art Metal company.

Plate 222. Candle Holders, chrome, 4″d, 1″h, stylized fish form handles.

Plate 223. Candle Holders and Nut Dish, 3½″h, chrome, blue mirror base, made by Chase Manufacturing Company.

Plate 224. Centerpiece, Compote with Candle Holders attached to Tray marked "Farberware, Brooklyn, N.Y."

Plate 225. Centerpiece: Console Bowl, 8¼" x 3¼" with matching Candle Holders, chrome, unmarked.

Plate 226. Centerpiece, 9½"h, brass, abstract figures posed in dance position support bowl, ca. 1930's, unmarked.

Plate 227. Centerpiece, 12"d, copper bowl, pot metal nude figure holds bird bath frog, originally silver plated.

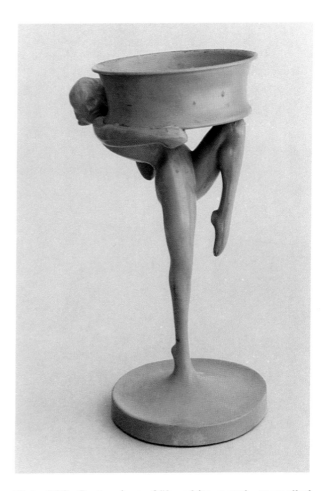

Plate 228. Centerpiece, 9"h, white metal, enamelled green finish, nude figure supports bowl, made by the Frankart Company.

Plate 229. Centerpiece, Console Bowl with flower frog, 11"l, "Tuscany" pattern by Roseville Pottery Company of Ohio.

Plate 230. Centerpiece Bowl, ceramic, 3"h, 11"d, black and green swag and tassel decor with woman's cameo outlined in black, triangle pierced work on border, unmarked, attributed to the Weller Pottery of Zanesville, Ohio.

Plate 231. Centerpiece Bowl, 17"d, blue glass, acid cut geometric designs, produced by the Daum factory in Nancy, France, signed.

Plate 232. Centerpiece Bowl, 7½"h, smoke colored glass molded with abstract leaf designs, square pedestal base, ca. 1930's, made by the Verlys Factory of Verlys, France.

Plate 233. Centerpiece Bowl, 9"h, free form shape, stepped base, unmarked.

Plate 234. Centerpiece Bowl, 6"h, 11"d, ceramic, diamond shape, stepped sides and base, orange, black and green handpainted work on white body, English, made by Myott & Son.

Plate 235. Centerpiece, 4"h, 7¼"d, light green glass, diamond shape, molded fan designs on body, pierced at top to hold flowers, unmarked.

Plate 236. Centerpiece Bowl, pink frosted glass, triangular shape with stepped base, handpainted black nude figure on each side. Originally the bowl would have had a pair of matching candle holders.

Plate 237. Centerpiece Frog, ceramic, 7″h, dancing nude figure, marked "Germany."

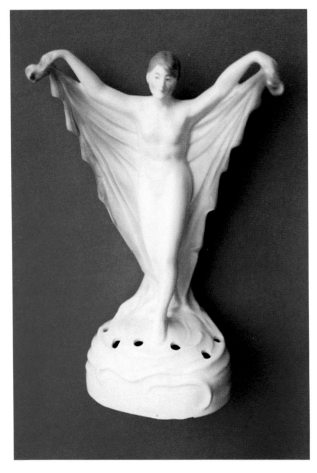

Plate 238. Centerpiece Frog, ceramic, 13½″h, nude figure holding full length veil, marked "Coronet," (American importer), made in Germany.

Plate 239. Centerpiece, 10″d, footed base, brass, silver and copper fashioned into abstract geometric designs, artist signed, made in Mexico.

Plate 240. Coffee Service, brass. The set includes Coffee Pot with warmer, Creamer, Sugar and Tray, ca. 1930's, marked ''Doryln Silversmith.''

Plate 241. Compote, 3½″h, 9¼″d, porcelain, handpainted silver butterflies on dark green background, artist signed, French Limoges porcelain, American decoration.

Plate 242. Compote, 3"h, 6½"d, porcelain, bold orange, black and white abstract designs on gold lustre background, Japanese, made by Noritake.

Plate 243. Covered Sugar Bowl, 5¼"h, porcelain, orange and yellow zig-zag design, lustre finish, Japanese.

Plate 244. Coffee Pot, copper, 13"h, wooden handle and finial, American.

Plate 245. Covered Butter Dish, 7½"l, 3½"h, made by the Hall China Company, East Liverpool, Ohio.

Plate 246. Cereal or Soup Bowl, 6"d and Cracker Jar, 7"h, porcelain, orange and yellow flowers on blue background, lustre finish, Japanese.

Plate 247. Creamer and Sugar Set on handled Tray, made by the Cambridge Glass Company of Ohio.

Plate 248. Creamer and Sugar Set on handled Tray, "Pyramid" pattern made by the Indiana Glass Company, ca. late 1920's.

Plate 249. Cup and Saucer, ceramic, triangular shape, "Tricorn" pattern made by the Salem China Company, Salem, Ohio.

Plate 250. Demi-tasse Cup and Saucer, ceramic, red, blue and green handpainted dots on cream colored background, black trim, "Ivory Ware" by Hancock Pottery, England.

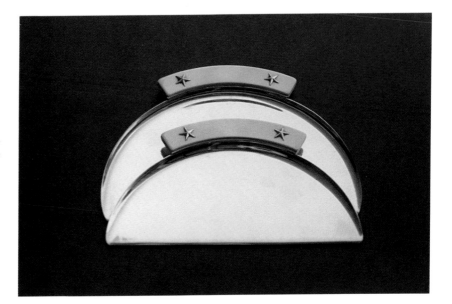

Plate 251. Crumber Set, chrome, celluloid trim, crescent moon shape, made by the Chase company.

Plate 252. Crumber Set, chrome, black trim, unmarked, attributed to Chase.

Plate 253. Creamer and Sugar with Tray, chrome, black bakelite handles, made by the Manning Bowman Co., Meriden, Connecticut.

Plate 254. Gravy Boat, "Fiesta," made by Homer Laughlin Pottery of Newell, West Virginia.

Plate 255. Flatware, Salad Fork and Spoon, chrome and celluloid, made by Chase.

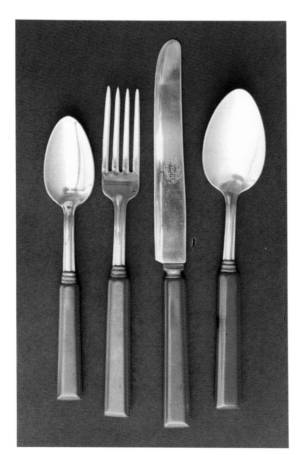

Plate 256. Flatware Place Setting, stainless steel with red bakelite handles.

Plate 257. Covered Pitchers, 16"h and 6"h, matching Tray, 12'l, ceramic, green glaze, molded leaf decor, made by Red Wing Pottery.

Plate 258. Water Pitcher, 7½"h, made by the Alamo Pottery of San Antonio, Texas.

Plate 259. Pitcher, 7"h, ceramic, off-white glaze, made by the Red Wing Pottery, Red Wing, Minnesota, ca. 1930's.

Plate 260. Pitcher, 7"h, porcelain, penguin figure, made by the Theodore Haviland Company, Limoges, France; signed by Edouard Sandoz, French artist noted for his Art Deco animal figures in porcelain and bronze, ca. 1920's. Other table figures designed by Sandoz for Haviland included ducks, fish and monkeys.

Plate 261. Cake Plate with matching Covered Creamer and Sugar, Bavarian and Limoges porcelain blanks hand-painted by the Juh H. Brauer Studio of Chicago.

Plate 262. Plate, 9"d, ceramic, facial profiles and crossed branches outlined in dark green, made by the Iroquois China Company.

Plate 263. Soup Bowl, ceramic, rectangular shape, orange and black inner line border, marked "The Biarritz, Royal Staffordshire Pottery, England."

Plate 264. Plate, 8¼"d, "Dance of the Nudes," made by the Consolidated Glass Company of Pennsylvania, ca. 1928.

Plate 265. Relish Dish, divided, light green glass, chrome triangular shaped holder with figural nudes at each corner, product of the Cambridge Glass Company of Ohio.

Plate 266. This and the following picture show various Deco designs in Salt and Pepper Shakers, ceramic, 3″ to 3½″h, American.

Plate 267. Salt and Pepper Shakers.

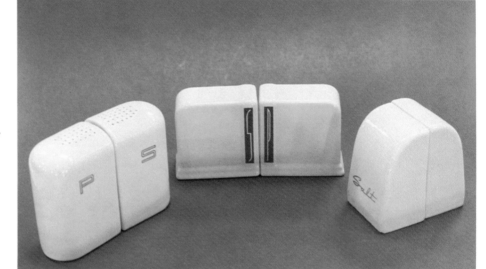

Plate 268. Serving Bowl, "Manhattan" pattern by the Anchor Hocking Glass Factory of Ohio, ca. late 1930's.

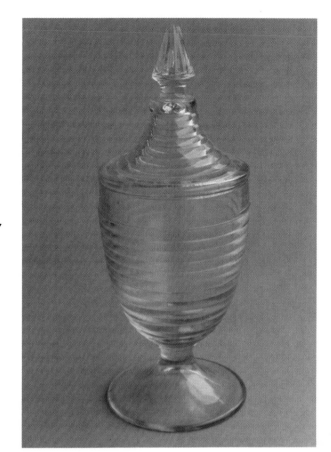

Plate 269. Covered Candy Jar, "Manhattan" pattern.

Plate 270. Serving Bowl, 8¼"d, three sections, "Square" design by the Cambridge Glass Company.

Plate 271. Serving Bowl, 12"d, "Windsor Diamond" pattern in pink, made by the Jeanette Glass Company.

Plate 272. Serving Bowl, 10½"l, black and multi-colored leaves on orange background, lustre finish, gold trim, Japanese.

Plate 273. Covered Serving Bowl, 8"d, "Fiesta" pattern in turquoise, made by the Homer Laughlin Pottery.

Plate 274. Teapot, 12½"l, ceramic, yellow glaze, "Ringware" pattern made by the Bauer Pottery of Los Angeles.

Plate 275. Teapot, 7½"h, yellow glaze with gold trim, "Modern" pattern made by the Hall China Company.

Plate 276. Teapot, 8½"h, ceramic, white glaze, orange herons made by the Hall China Company.

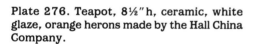

Plate 277. Covered Syrup Pitcher, 6"h, amber glass, "Mayfair" pattern made by the Fostoria Glass Company of West Virginia.

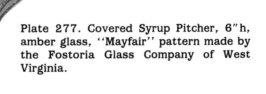

Plate 278. Electric Toaster, chrome, black trim, made by Sunbeam.

Vases

Vases are designed for displaying floral arrangements, but as solitary objects they enhance a room's decor. Instead of being merely flower containers, they are considered art objects or decorative accessories, depending on their price. Like table wares, Deco vases were made of either pottery, porcelain, glass or metal. The photographs in this section are arranged in that order.

French art glass vases are the most expensive. Examples shown here include pieces by Legras, Schneider and Verlys. Other French manufacturers such as Baccarat, Lalique and Gallé perhaps are more famous. But as their creations have become scarce and very costly, other factories' products have gained recognition. Consequently, most French art glass has moved entirely out of the range of the moderate collector.

For Deco image, however, less expensive vases made by European and American factories are quite pleasing. Much of this glass is unmarked and not attributable to any one factory. Lack of identification may serve the collector well when Deco shape rather than company or artist is the major concern. Czechoslovakian glass made between 1918 and 1939 has been gaining interest among Deco collectors for several years. Most of the pieces are marked "Czechoslovakia" or "Made in Czechoslovakia." The shapes and vivid colors of this good quality glass are quite representative of the Deco era. Prices usually remain moderate. Black milk glass or black amethyst glass made during the 1920's and 1930's is another type of relatively inexpensive glass with Deco overtones. Black glass was made by several American factories, but most pieces are unmarked.

American glass makers such as Cambridge, Fostoria, Heisey and New Martinsville, to name a few, are noted for stemware and serving dishes, but vases and other decorative items also were produced by these factories. Clear and colored glass vases were sometimes made to match the modern table ware patterns. Fan shapes, blocked geometric forms and even etched nude designs project a Deco theme. Although this type of glass is avidly collected by Depression glass collectors, prices are far less than those for French art glass.

The most expensive ceramic vases are those made by European art potteries. Art pottery, however, usually is priced lower than art glass. This is apparent when prices are compared for the Amphora and Boch Freres ceramic vases with those for the Legras and Verlys glass examples. American art pottery is generally lower in price than European. Among American Art potteries, attention is being paid to the Deco production made by companies such as Roseville. Less expensive vases are Japanese or American pottery varieties which were sold by dime stores or florists' shops. The angular white glazed Japanese vase shown here was originally cheap, but the striking Deco shape has caused its current value to increase sharply.

Porcelain vases are medium priced with few being either bargains or exorbitantly high. Porcelain is superior to simple pottery because it is stronger and translucent, but those qualities are not always reflected in prices. Most European porcelain vases are less expensive than European art pottery. The reason is because many decorative items such as urns, vases and jardinieres were produced in quantity by porcelain factories. Moreover, they were often decorated with transfer designs or exported as undecorated vases. The latter were purchased by aspiring amateur china painters, and thus the decoration is not as creative or professional as that of art potteries.

Metal adapts well to angular shapes. Although glass and ceramic vases are more common, those made of brass, bronze, copper or chrome often evoke the Deco image in a more eye-catching way. The chrome vases pictured here are priced at the low end of the scale, but the Deco features are quite obvious. Brass and copper vases vary in price depending on size, but most are over $100. The sterling on bronze vases were made by the Heintz Art Metal Company. Such pieces are rarely less than $100 or more than $300. French bronze vases may be out of an affordable price range for moderate collectors. But an urn like the one shown, or similar vases, is usually considerably less than a bronze statue would cost. If French bronze would lend a note of prestige to one's collection, such vases are a good choice.

Plate 279. Wall Pocket Vase, pottery, woman's head with large hat, white glaze, unmarked.

Plate 280. Vase, 7″h, pottery, white glaze, marked "Made in Japan."

Plate 281. Vase, 6½″h, 5½″w, pottery, stylized wild duck molded in relief on front with cactus plant incised on reverse (not shown), honey tan glaze, made by the Frankoma Pottery of Salpulpa, Oklahoma, ca. 1930's.

Plate 282. Pair of Vases, 11″h, pottery, stylized lily shape, dark green glaze, marked with "Camark" original paper label of the Camden Art and Tile Pottery of Camden, Arkansas.

Plate 283. Vase, 7"h, yellow pottery made by the Belgian Boch Freres factory, artist signed ''Lison.''

Plate 284. Vase, 14½"h, pottery, enamelled stylized flowers, marked "Amphora, Austria."

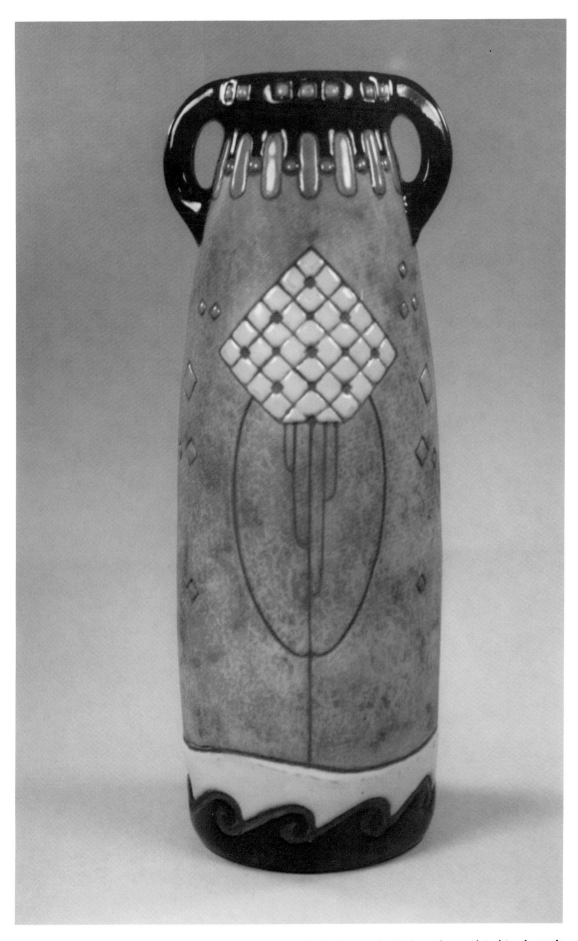

Plate 285. Vase, 13½" h, pottery, enamelled geometric designs, cobalt blue trim, artist signed, marked "Amphora, Made in Czechoslovakia."

Plate 286. Vase, 7"h, "Ivory" pattern by Roseville.

Plate 287. Planter, 7½" x 8", "Klyro" pattern made by Weller Pottery of Zanesville, Ohio.

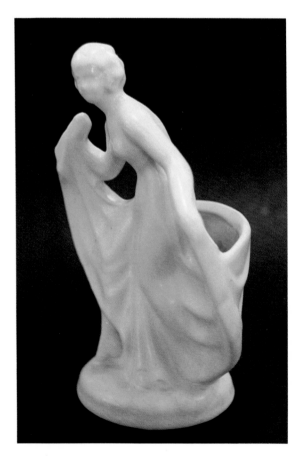

Plate 288. Figural Planter, 7½"h, nude figure with drape, "Hobart" line made by Weller Pottery.

Plate 289. Vase, 9″h, white glaze, made by the Abingdon Pottery, Abingdon, Illinois.

Plate 290. Vase, 8½″h, porcelain, handpainted by Brauer Art Studio, Egyptian motif.

Plate 291. Vase, 12″h, pottery, green and yellow abstract work on white body, made by Villeroy and Boch, Mettlach, Germany.

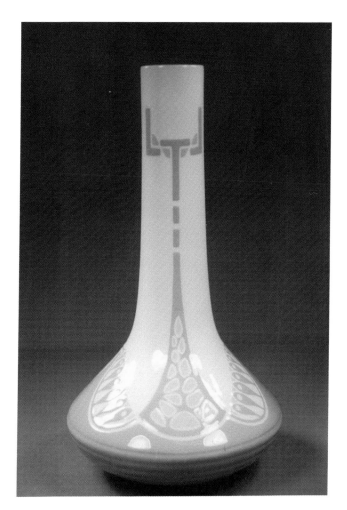

Plate 292. Vase, 4½"h, blue matte glaze, molded geometric designs, made by Roseville.

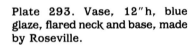

Plate 293. Vase, 12"h, blue glaze, flared neck and base, made by Roseville.

Plate 294. Vase, 8"h, pottery, zig-zagged lines form a flame design, made by the Ditmar Urbach Pottery, Czechoslovakia.

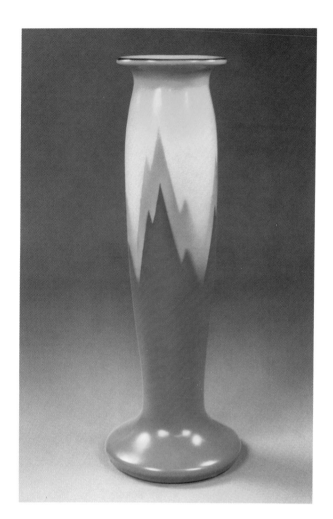

Plate 295. Vase, 12″ h, another flame decoration by the Ditmar Urbach Pottery.

Plate 296. Vase, 6½″ h, "Cornacopia" pattern made by New Martinsville Glass Company.

Plate 297. Vase. 6″ h, black amethyst glass, handpainted silver geometric decor, unmarked.

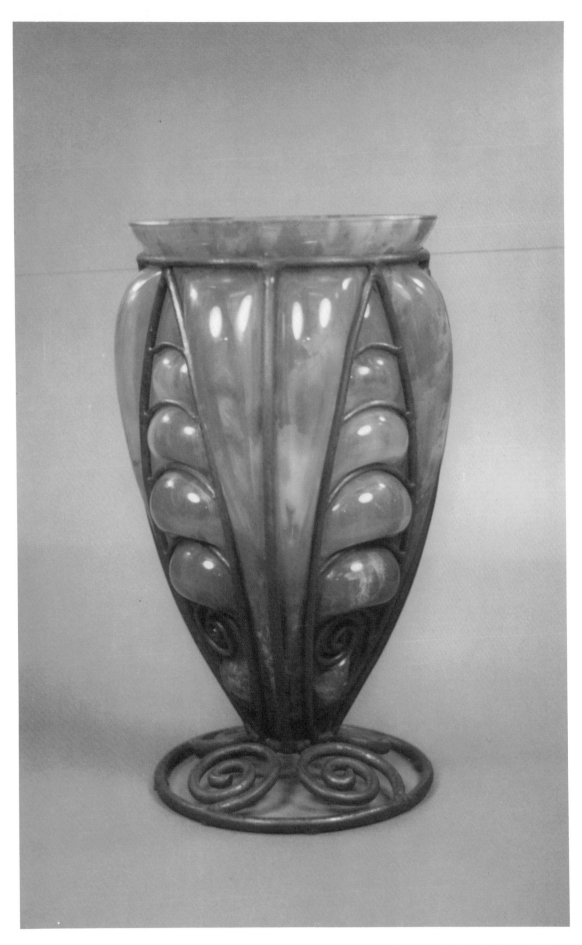

Plate 298. Vase, 12"h, blown blue-green glass encased in wrought iron, made by the Daum factory in Nancy, France.

Plate 299. Vase, 16"h, glass, modernistic design made by the Legras factory of St. Denis, France, prior to 1914 (the date the factory closed), artist signed.

Plate 300. Vase, 11"h, glass, molded leaf decor highlighted by handpainted blue-green interior, Czechoslovakian.

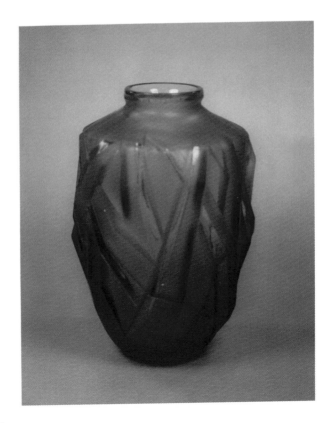

Plate 301. Vase, 8½"h, smoke glass molded with designs commemorating the Maginot Line from World War I, made by the Schneider Art Glass Factory of Epinany-sur-Seine, France.

121

Plate 302. Vase, 9″ h, light green glass, silver trim outlines legs and neck, unmarked.

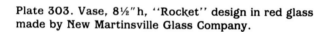

Plate 303. Vase, 8½″ h, ''Rocket'' design in red glass made by New Martinsville Glass Company.

Plate 304. Vase, 7″ h, black glass, triangle shaped neck, nude figures decorate base, made by the L.E. Smith Glass Company, Mt. Pleasant, Pennsylvania, ca. 1930's.

Plate 305. Vase, 12"h, black glass, trumpet shaped, unmarked.

Plate 306. Vase, 7½"h. satin glass, pink with black and white enamelled work, marked "Made in Czechoslovakia."

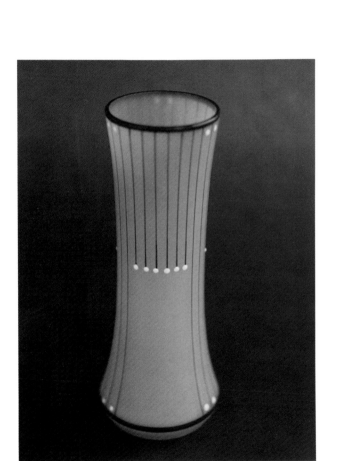

Plate 307. Vase, 9"h, dark green glass, Zepplin shaped base, unmarked.

Plate 308. Vase, 11½" h, vaseline glass in metal holder with dancing nude figure, made by Frankart.

Plate 309. Vase, 8″h, chrome, wall pocket, unmarked.

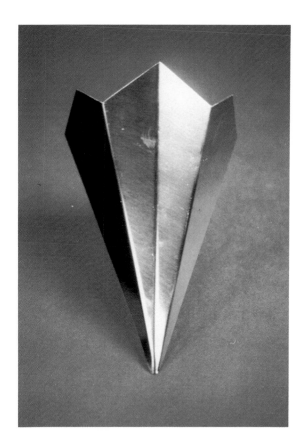

Plate 310. Vase, 8¼″h, chrome, hammered surface, unmarked.

Plate 311. Pair of Vases, 9″h, chrome, unmarked.

Plate 312. Pair of Vases, 8"h, hammered chrome, marked "Made in England."

Plate 313. Vase, 12"h, sterling on bronze made by the Heintz Art Metal Company of Buffalo, New York, stylized leaf designs.

Plate 314. Vase, 12"h, sterling on bronze made by the Heintz Company, geometric shaped roses and leaves.

Plate 316. Pair of Vases, 13″h, copper, Egyptian influence, ca. late 1920's.

Plate 315. Vase, 13″h, sterling on bronze made by Heintz, stylized chrysanthemums.

Plate 317. Urn, 8½″h, bronze, transitional elements of Art Nouveau and Art Deco, French.

Plate 318. Vase, 10½″ h, brass with silver overlay, abstract geometric pattern, artist signed ''George,'' French.

Index To Objects

Index To Manufacturers & Marks

Bibliography

Arwas, Victor, *Art Deco.* New York: Harry N. Abrams, Inc., 1980.

Baker, Lillian. *Art Nouveau & Art Deco Jewelry.* Paducah, Kentucky: Collector Books, 1981.

Blasberg, Robert W. and Carol L. Bohdan. *Fulper Art Pottery.* New York: The Jordan-Volpe Gallery, n.d.

Battersby, Martin, *The Decorative Twenties.* New York: Walker and Company, 1969.

Brunhammer, Yvonne. *The Nineteen Twenties Style.* London: Paul Hamlyn, 1969.

Duncan, Alastair. *Art Deco Furniture and the French Designers.* New York: Holt, Rinehart and Winston, 1984.

Florence, Gene. *The Collector's Encyclopedia of Depression Glass.* Paducah, Kentucky: Collector Books, 1979.

_____. *Elegant Glassware of the Depression Era.* Paducah, Kentucky: Collector Books, 1983.

Forsythe, Ruth A. *Made in Czechoslovakia.* Galena, Ohio: Ruth A. Forsythe, 1982.

Fredgant, Don. *Collecting Art Nouveau: Identification and Value Guide.* Florence, Alabama; Books Americana, 1982.

Gaston, Mary Frank. *Antique Brass.* Paducah, Kentucky: Collector Books, 1985.

_____. *Antique Copper.* Paducah, Kentucky: Collector Books, 1985.

_____. *Haviland Collectables and Objects of Art.* Paducah, Kentucky: Collector Books, 1984.

Godden, Geoffrey. *Encylcopedia of British Pottery and Porcelain Marks.* New York: Crown Publishers, 1964.

Greif, Martin. *Depression Modern: The Thirties Style in America.* New York, Universe Books, 1975.

Hillier, Bevis. *Art Deco of the 20's and 30's* (rev. ed.). New York: Schocken Books, 1985.

_____. *Minneapolis Institute of the Arts Catalog: The World of Art Deco.* New York: E.P. Dutton, 1971.

_____. *The Decorative Arts of the Forties and Fifties.* New York: Clarkson N. Potter, Inc., 1975.

Hull, John. *Art Deco.* San Francisco: Troubador Press, 1975.

Huxford, Sharon and Bob (eds.). *Schroeder's Antiques Price Guide.* Paducah, Kentucky: Collector Books, 1988.

Jervis, Simon. *The Facts on File: Dictionary of Design and Designers.* New York: Facts on File, Inc., 1984.

Klein, Dan. *Art Deco.* London: Treasure Press, 1984.

Kovel, Ralph and Terry. *The Kovel's Antiques & Collectibles Price List.* New York: Crown Publishers, Inc., 1987.

Lehner, Lois. *Ohio Pottery and Glass Marks and Manufacturers.* Des Moines, Iowa; Wallace-Homestead Book Co., 1978.

Lesieutre, Alain. *The Spirit and Splendor of Art Deco.* New York: Paddington Press Ltd., 1974.

McClinton, Katherine Morrison. *Art Deco: A Guide for Collectors.* New York: Clarkson N. Potter, Inc., 1972; rev. ed. 1986.

Maenz, Paul. *Art Deco 1920-1940.* Koln: Verlag M. DuMont, 1974.

Menten, Theodore. *The Art Deco Style.* New York: Dover Publications, Inc., 1972.

_____. *Advertising Art in the Art Deco Style.* New York: Dover Publications, Inc., 1975.

Miller, Martin and Judith. *Miller's Antiques Price Guide.* Cranbrook, England: M.J.M. Publications, Ltd., 1985.

Murphy, Catherine and Kyle Husfloen (eds.). *The Antique Trader Antiques and Collectibles Price Guide.* Dubuque, Iowa: Babka Publishing Co., 1987.

Röntgen, Robert E. *Marks on German, Bohemian and Austrian Porcelain: 1710 to present.* Exton, Pennsylvania: Schiffer Publishing Co., 1981.

Scarlett, Frank and Marjorie Townley. *Arts Decoratifs 1925.* London: St. Martin's Press, 1975.

Sembach, Klaus Jorgen. *Style 1930.* New York: Universe Books, 1971.

Veronesi, Giulia. *Style and Design 1909-1929.* New York: George Braziller, 1968.

Warman's 1987 Antiques and Their Prices. Willow Grove, Pennsylvania: Warman Publishing Co., Inc., 1987.

Weinstein, Iris and Robert K. Brown. *Art Deco Internationale.* New York: Quick Fox, 1977.

Woodard, Dannie A. and Billie J. Wood. *Hammered Aluminum Hand Wrought Collectibles.* Wolfe City, Texas: Henington Publishing Co., 1983.

Price Guide

Plate 1	$30.00-40.00
Plate 2	$700.00-800.00
Plate 3	see Plate 2
Plate 4	$120.00-140.00
Plate 5	$250.00-275.00
Plate 6	$20.00-30.00
Plate 7	$15.00-20.00
Plate 8	$15.00-20.00
Plate 9	each $10.00-12.00
Plate 10	each $12.00-15.00
Plate 11	$100.00-120.00
Plate 12	each $8.00-12.00
Plate 13	each $50.00-60.00
Plate 14	$20.00-30.00
Plate 15	$25.00-35.00
Plate 16	$30.00-40.00
Plate 17	$40.00-50.00
Plate 18	each $35.00-45.00
Plate 19	each $100.00-125.00
Plate 20	set $70.00-80.00
Plate 21	set $225.00-250.00
Plate 22	$65.00-75.00
Plate 23	$50.00-75.00
Plate 24	$600.00-700.00
Plate 25	set $250.00-300.00
Plate 26	set $900.00-1,000.00
Plate 27	set $450.00-550.00
Plate 28	$120.00-140.00
Plate 29	$550.00-650.00
Plate 30	$150.00-175.00
Plate 31	$175.00-250.00
Plate 32	$100.00-125.00
Plate 33	$80.00-100.00
Plate 34	$150.00-175.00
Plate 35	$125.00-150.00
Plate 36	$150.00-175.00
Plate 37	$150.00-175.00
Plate 38	$350.00-400.00
Plate 39	$375.00-425.00
Plate 40	$80.00-100.00
Plate 41	$100.00-125.00
Plate 42	$85.00-95.00
Plate 43	$50.00-60.00
Plate 44	$55.00-65.00
Plate 45	$90.00-100.00
Plate 46	$90.00-100.00
Plate 47, top	$120.00-140.00
left	$45.00-55.00
right	$45.00-55.00
Plate 48	$30.00-40.00
Plate 49	$70.00-80.00
Plate 50	$75.00-85.00
Plate 51	$60.00-70.00
Plate 52	$12.00-15.00
Plate 53	each $6.00-12.00
Plate 54	$12.00-15.00
Plate 55	$175.00-225.00
Plate 56	$60.00-70.00
Plate 57	$15.00-18.00
Plate 58	pair $25.00-30.00
Plate 59	$25.00-30.00
Plate 60	$90.00-100.00
Plate 61	set $800.00-900.00
Plate 62	$70.00-80.00
Plate 63, top	$25.00-30.00
others	$20.00-25.00
Plate 64	each $30.00-40.00
Plate 65, left	$25.00-30.00
right	$30.00-35.00
Plate 66	set $40.00-50.00
Plate 67	set $1,200.00-1,400.00
Plate 68	$40.00-45.00
Plate 69, top	$175.00-225.00
middle	$150.00-175.00
bottom	$30.00-40.00
Plate 70	$10.00-12.00
Plate 71	$30.00-35.00
Plate 72	$80.00-100.00
Plate 73, top	$80.00-100.00
left	$160.00-180.00
right	$80.00-100.00
Plate 74	$30.00-40.00
Plate 75	$12.00-15.00
Plate 76	$30.00-35.00
Plate 77	$30.00-35.00
Plate 78	$35.00-40.00
Plate 79	$100.00-125.00
Plate 80	set $35.00-45.00
Plate 81	$6.00-8.00
Plate 82	$20.00-25.00
Plate 83	$150.00-175.00
Plate 84	$225.00-250.00
Plate 85	$45.00-55.00
Plate 86	set $140.00-160.00
Plate 87	set $150.00-200.00
Plate 88	see Plate 87
Plate 89	set $50.00-60.00
Plate 90	set $60.00-80.00
Plate 91	$65.00-75.00
Plate 92	$120.00-130.00
Plate 93	$70.00-80.00
Plate 94	pair $400.00-450.00
Plate 95	$45.00-55.00
Plate 96	$40.00-50.00
Plate 97	$8.00-12.00
Plate 98	$50.00-60.00
Plate 99	$65.00-75.00
Plate 100	$175.00-200.00
Plate 101	$65.00-75.00
Plate 102	$125.00-150.00

Plate 103 . . . . $250.00-300.00
Plate 104 . . . . $90.00-110.00
Plate 105 . . . . $200.00-225.00
Plate 106 . . . . $125.00-150.00
Plate 107 . . . . $150.00-175.00
Plate 108 . . . . $225.00-275.00
Plate 109 . . . . $1,500.00-1,800.00
Plate 110 . . . . pair $350.00-400.00
Plate 111 . . . . $1,100.00-1,300.00
Plate 112 . . . . $125.00-150.00
Plate 113 . . . . $225.00-250.00
Plate 114 . . . . $1,800.00-2,000.00
Plate 115 . . . . $100.00-120.00
Plate 116 . . . . $20.00-25.00
Plate 117 . . . . $175.00-200.00
Plate 118 . . . . $1,800.00-2,000.00
Plate 119 . . . . pair $80.00-100.00
Plate 120 . . . . $400.00-500.00
Plate 121 . . . . pair $80.00-100.00
Plate 122 . . . . pair $160.00-180.00
Plate 123 . . . . each $20.00-30.00
Plate 124 . . . . pair $50.00-60.00
Plate 125 . . . . $30.00-35.00
Plate 126 . . . . pair $150.00-175.00
Plate 127 . . . . pair $100.00-125.00
Plate 128 . . . . set $250.00-275.00
Plate 129 . . . . see Plate 128
Plate 130 . . . . set $80.00-100.00
Plate 131 . . . . $250.00-275.00
Plate 132 . . . . $80.00-100.00
Plate 133 . . . . $60.00-80.00
Plate 134 . . . . $75.00-85.00
Plate 135 . . . . $100.00-125.00
Plate 136 . . . . (frame only) $45.00-55.00
Plate 137 . . . . $20.00-25.00
Plate 138 . . . . $500.00-600.00
Plate 139 . . . . $125.00-150.00
Plate 140 . . . . $1,000.00-1,200.00
Plate 141 . . . . $150.00-200.00
Plate 142 . . . . $125.00-150.00
Plate 143 . . . . $125.00-150.00
Plate 144 . . . . $75.00-100.00
Plate 145 . . . . $500.00-600.00
Plate 146 . . . . $40.00-50.00
Plate 147 . . . . $20.00-25.00
Plate 148 . . . . $25.00-35.00
Plate 149 . . . . $100.00-125.00
Plate 150 . . . . each $6.00-8.00
Plate 151, top $10.00-12.00
    bottom . . . . each $8.00-10.00
Plate 152 . . . . $70.00-80.00
Plate 153 . . . . $80.00-100.00
Plate 154 . . . . $20.00-25.00
Plate 155 . . . . set $100.00-120.00
Plate 156 . . . . $75.00-85.00
Plate 157 . . . . set $60.00-70.00
Plate 158 . . . . $10.00-12.00
Plate 159 . . . . $20.00-25.00
Plate 160 . . . . $25.00-30.00
Plate 161, left $30.00-35.00
    right $25.00-30.00
Plate 162 . . . . $35.00-40.00
Plate 163 . . . . $25.00-30.00
Plate 164 . . . . $25.00-30.00
Plate 165 . . . . $125.00-150.00

Plate 166 . . . . $8.00-10.00
Plate 167 . . . . $25.00-30.00
Plate 168 . . . . $50.00-60.00
Plate 169 . . . . $80.00-100.00
Plate 170 . . . . $125.00-150.00
Plate 171 . . . . $100.00-125.00
Plate 172 . . . . $40.00-50.00
Plate 173 . . . . $65.00-85.00
Plate 174 . . . . each $10.00-14.00
Plate 175 . . . . each $8.00-12.00
Plate 176 . . . . each $8.00-14.00
Plate 177 . . . . $70.00-80.00
Plate 178, tortoise $30.00-40.00
    white $35.00-45.00
    red $45.00-55.00
Plate 179 . . . . $35.00-45.00
Plate 180, gold $80.00-100.00
    white $120.00-140.00
Plate 181 . . . . $1,200.00-1,400.00
Plate 182 . . . . see Plate 181
Plate 183 . . . . $100.00-125.00
Plate 184 . . . . $100.00-125.00
Plate 185 . . . . $60.00-80.00
Plate 186 . . . . $100.00-125.00
Plate 187 . . . . $100.00-125.00
Plate 188 . . . . $125.00-150.00
Plate 189 . . . . $350.00-400.00
Plate 190 . . . . $225.00-250.00
Plate 191 . . . . $80.00-100.00
Plate 192 . . . . $250.00-275.00
Plate 193 . . . . $500.00-600.00
Plate 194 . . . . $400.00-500.00
Plate 195 . . . . $150.00-175.00
Plate 196 . . . . $125.00-150.00
Plate 197 . . . . $100.00-150.00
Plate 198 . . . . $250.00-300.00
Plate 199 . . . . $125.00-150.00
Plate 200 . . . . $225.00-275.00
Plate 201 . . . . $80.00-100.00
Plate 202 . . . . $125.00-150.00
Plate 203 . . . . $200.00-250.00
Plate 204 . . . . $700.00-800.00
Plate 205 . . . . $600.00-700.00
Plate 206 . . . . $225.00-275.00
Plate 207 . . . . $200.00-250.00
Plate 208 . . . . $600.00-700.00
Plate 209 . . . . $100.00-125.00
Plate 210 . . . . $400.00-500.00
Plate 211 . . . . $200.00-250.00
Plate 212 . . . . $250.00-300.00
Plate 213 . . . . $150.00-200.00
Plate 214 . . . . $1,000.00-1,200.00
Plate 215 . . . . $350.00-450.00
Plate 216 . . . . $60.00-80.00
Plate 217 . . . . $30.00-40.00
Plate 218 . . . . $25.00-30.00
Plate 219 . . . . pair $60.00-70.00
Plate 220 . . . . pair $125.00-150.00
Plate 221 . . . . pair $125.00-150.00
Plate 222 . . . . pair $30.00-35.00
Plate 223 . . . . set $80.00-100.00
Plate 224 . . . . set $100.00-125.00
Plate 225 . . . . set $80.00-100.00
Plate 226 . . . . $125.00-150.00
Plate 227 . . . . $250.00-300.00

Schroeder's Antiques Price Guide

Schroeder's Antiques Price Guide has climbed its way to the top in a field already supplied with several well-established publications! The word is out, *Schroeder's Price Guide* is the best buy at any price. Over 500 categories are covered, with more than 50,000 listings. But it's not volume alone that makes Schroeder's the unique guide it is recognized to be. From ABC Plates to Zsolnay, if it merits the interest of today's collector, you'll find it in Schroeder's. Each subject is represented with histories and background information. In addition, hundreds of sharp original photos are used each year to illustrate not only the rare and the unusual, but the everyday "fun-type" collectibles as well -- not postage stamp pictures, but large close-up shots that show important details clearly.

Each edition is completely re-typeset from all new sources. We have not and will not simply change prices in each new edition. All new copy and all new illustrations make Schroeder's THE price guide on antiques and collectibles.

The writing and researching team behind this giant is proportionately large. It is backed by a staff of more than seventy of Collector Books' finest authors, as well as a board of advisors made up of well-known antique authorities and the country's top dealers, all specialists in their fields. Accuracy is their primary aim. Prices are gathered over the entire year previous to publication, from ads and personal contacts. Then each category is thoroughly checked to spot inconsistencies, listings that may not be entirely reflective of actual market dealings, and lines too vague to be of merit.

Only the best of the lot remains for publication. You'll find *Schroeder's Antiques Price Guide* the one to buy for factual information and quality.

No dealer, collector or investor can afford not to own this book. It is available from your favorite bookseller or antiques dealer at the low price of $12.95. If you are unable to find this price guide in your area, it's available from Collector Books, P. O. Box 3009, Paducah, KY 42001 at $12.95 plus $2.00 for postage and handling.

8½ x 11, 608 Pages $12.95